# Sew Quick
## Sew Cute

### Fiona Goble

**A** adams media

Published by
Adams Media, a division of F+W Media, Inc.
57 Littlefield Street, Avon, MA 02322. U.S.A.
www.adamsmedia.com

ISBN-10: 1-4405-6520-1
ISBN-13: 978-1-4405-6520-5
eISBN-10: 1-4405-6521-X
eISBN-13: 978-1-4405-6521-2

Printed in China
Color origination by Ivy Press Reprographics

10 9 8 7 6 5 4 3 2 1

**Library of Congress Cataloging-in-Publication Data**
is available from the publisher.

This book was conceived, designed, and produced by
**Ivy Press**
*Creative Director*  Peter Bridgewater
*Publisher*  Susan Kelly
*Commissioning Editor*  Sophie Collins
*Editorial Director*  Tom Kitch
*Art Director*  James Lawrence
*Design*  JC Lanaway
*Photographer*  Neal Grundy
*Illustrator*  Cathy Brear
*Models*  Arthur Anderson, Grace Anderson, Hannah Coulson, Ava James, Edd Lawrence, Koren Livesey, Lola Moore, Elodie Moore, Emily Owen, Sophia Retief and Amy Sewell

*This book is available at quantity discounts for bulk purchases.*
*For information, please call 1-800-289-0963.*

# Contents

# Introduction

This book was written with the busy sewer in mind. The techniques are straightforward, with detailed step sequences so you can learn as you go or easily skip anything you know already. Some projects will take no more than a couple of hours, and nothing takes longer than a weekend.

## Stock up your sewing basket

Before you get going on your first project, you will need to make sure you have got everything you need. You will almost certainly have some of these items already, but there might be a few that you will need to buy.

## Buying a sewing machine

If you are buying a new sewing machine, I recommend that you get a mid-priced one if you are planning to do a lot of sewing. It will almost certainly last longer, run more smoothly, and be less noisy than a budget model.

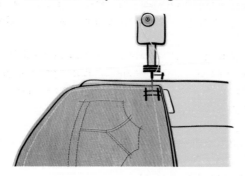

**Sewing machine** A simple machine that does straight stitch and zigzag stitch is all you'll need.

**Sewing machine needles** Most of the projects in this book require a standard needle for sewing medium-weight fabrics. Change your needle frequently.

**Dressmaking scissors** For cutting only fabric.

**Small scissors** For trimming threads, cutting out very small fabric pieces, etc.

**Ordinary scissors** For cutting paper templates.

**Hand sewing needles** For some projects, you will also need an embroidery needle.

**Straight pins** For some projects, you may also need quilter's pins.

**Stitch ripper and tweezers**

**Tape measure**

**Safety pins**

**Iron and ironing board**

**Fabric marking pen and quilter's pencil**

# Material world

There are several different types of fabrics and other sewing items that are used in the projects. The main ones are listed below.

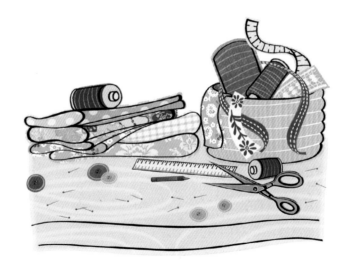

**Cotton** Most of the cotton fabrics in this book are medium-weight woven cottons, suitable for dressmaking and patchwork. Quilting fabrics are a great choice because they are available in small amounts and come in a huge variety of patterns. Remember to wash your fabric before use if it has not been preshrunken.

**Polyester fleece** The fleece fabric is usually mid-weight and is soft, and it is a little stretchy. Because it is textured, it does not slip around too much and is easy to sew, even for beginners. You do not need to wash fleece before sewing because it does not shrink.

**Felt** Felt is a firm, nonwoven fabric that is easy to sew and doesn't fray. If possible, try to buy felt that contains a percentage of wool, because it is much nicer than the 100 percent acrylic versions and only costs a little bit more.

**Fusible web** Fusible web (sometimes called fusible bonding web) is a thin web of glue, with paper on one side. It can be used to create fabric appliqués or to bond different pieces of fabric together.

## You will also need

Elastic, ribbons, cord, braid, and buttons for some of the projects featured in this book.

**Polyester fiber filling** Polyester filling (or stuffing) is a collection of fluffy white fibers used for stuffing toys and other handmade items. Make sure that the one you buy conforms to relevant safety standards.

**Polyester batting** Polyester batting is a little like a sheet of polyester fiber filling and is usually used as a lightweight interlining for quilts and other padded handmade items. It is sewn in between the front and backing fabrics.

**Cotton batting** Cotton batting is used to interline fabrics to give them a bit more substance and weight. It is denser and flatter than polyester batting.

**Iron-on fusible interfacing** This is available in different weights or thicknesses. It is ironed onto the reverse of your fabric to make it stiffer and more substantial.

**Threads** All-purpose polyester threads are ideal for the projects in this book and come in a great range of colors. Choose a good quality thread because cheap ones tend to snap and tangle.

**Tacky glue** This is a special kind of polyvinyl acetate (PVA) glue that is slightly thicker and easier to work with than standard PVA.

# Know the basics

There are a few basic techniques you will need to know to make sure your projects come together easily and look professional.

**Preparing your templates** Many of the projects will require you to use the templates provided. While it's possible to copy them by hand, it's more accurate to use a photocopier or a computer with a scanner.

To use a photocopier, simply set the copier to enlarge by the percentage listed and make a copy. If the template will be too large for the paper you are using, you will need to copy different areas and then attach the pieces together using tape. You may want to add marks to the pattern, which you can use to align the individual pieces of paper with each other.

If you are using a scanner and a computer, resize your scan to the size indicated on the pattern, using your graphics editing software, and then print out the scan. If the enlarged pattern is too big for your printer's paper, depending on your software and printer, you may have the option for "tiling," in which case the template will be printed on multiple sheets that can be pieced together and attached with tape. If tiling isn't an option, you may need to divide the template into smaller sections manually, print them out onto individual sheets, and then piece them together and attach them with tape.

**Using fusible web to create an appliqué shape** Fusible web is a thin web of glue on a paper backing. To use it to create an appliqué, first trace or draw your shape onto the paper side of the fusible web, using an ordinary pencil. Cut the shape out roughly, then iron the fusible web glue side down onto the reverse of your appliqué fabric. Cut the shape out and carefully peel off the paper backing. Position the appliqué on your item and iron in place before sewing.

**Using fusible web to line or layer fabrics** You can also use fusible web to adhere backing fabric to a main piece of fabric. To do this, simply iron the relevant size piece of fusible web to the reverse of one piece of fabric. Then peel off the backing paper and iron the fabric, fusible web side down, onto the reverse of your second piece of fabric.

**Cutting on the bias** If you look closely at a woven fabric, such as woven cotton, you will see lines of thread running across and up and down the fabric. This is called the "grain" of the fabric. Cutting on the bias means cutting across the grain, at an angle of 45 degrees. So to cut a piece on the bias, you will need to lay the template diagonally on your fabric. Pieces cut on the bias will have more flow and stretch than pieces cut in the usual way.

Cutting on the bias

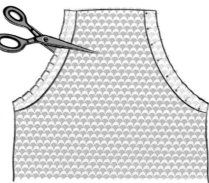

Clipping curves

Topstitch

**Clipping curves** When you sew a curved seam on a woven fabric, you may need to make small cuts into the seam allowance so that the seam on your finished item lies flat. Use small scissors and be careful that you do not cut into your seam.

**Clipping corners** When you sew a seam around a corner, it's a good idea to clip off the tip of the corner on the seam allowance. This reduces the bulk of the seam and helps make the corner look pointy. Be careful that you don't cut too near the seam.

**Securing your stitches** When you are machine stitching, work a few stitches back and forth to secure your thread at the beginning and end of your seams. When you are hand stitching, tie a knot in your thread and work two or three stitches, one over the other, when starting your work. You will also need to work a few stitches, one over the other, to secure your thread once you have finished.

**Topstitch** Topstitch is simply a line of normal machine stitching that runs parallel to an edge or a seam. It helps give items a professional finish and often also helps to hold the item's shape.

**Running stitch** This is the simplest stitch of all and involves taking your needle in and out of your work at regular intervals. You may need to practice to make sure your stitches and the gaps between them are nice and regular.

**Tacking** Tacking, sometimes called "basting," is a temporary stitch used to keep your fabric in place while you work your permanent stitching. Tacking stitches are really just big running stitches. It doesn't matter what they look like, as long as they do the job, because you will remove them once your project is complete.

**Slip stitch** Slip stitch is used to sew up the gaps that have been used for turning and stuffing. Fold the raw edges of the gap to the inside, in line with the seam. Run your needle about ⅛ inch (3 mm) inside the fold on one side then straight across to the inside of the fold of the other side. Repeat, working back and forth, until you come to the end of the gap.

**Overcasting** Overcasting is worked along the edge of a piece of fabric. You simply take your thread over the edge of the fabric then back out again about ⅛ inch (3 mm) farther along.

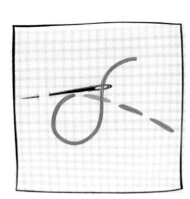

Running stitch

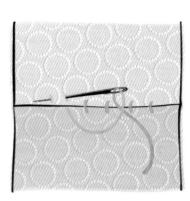

Slip stitch

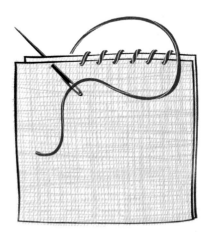

Overcasting

# Tomato pincushion

If you're dipping your toe into the world of sewing for the first time, a pincushion is a good first project: easy *and* useful. The design is an update on a nineteenth-centry British classic—at the time, domestic accessories were often tomato shaped, because a "lucky" tomato on the mantelpiece of a new home was believed to bring prosperity. We've added a handful of rice in the bottom to give it weight and keep it upright. The pincushion is about 2½ inches (6 cm) high.

## You will need

- ✕ Template on page 10
- ✕ Tracing paper and paper for template
- ✕ Pencil
- ✕ Scrap of green felt
- ✕ 4¾ x 9½-inch (12 x 24 cm) cotton fabric cut on the bias
- ✕ Green sewing thread
- ✕ Thread to match your fabric
- ✕ Handful of rice or lentils (optional)
- ✕ Handful of polyester fiber filling
- ✕ Basic sewing kit (see page 4)
- ✕ Fabric marking pen

# How to make the tomato pincushion

{1} Using the template below, cut out the leaf shape from green felt and cut out a ¾ x 1⅛-inch (2 x 3-cm) rectangle of felt for the stem.

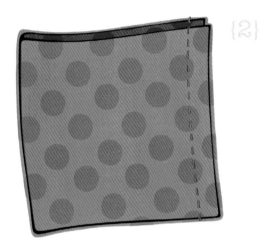

{2} Check that your main fabric has been cut on the bias (see page 6). Fold your main fabric in half widthwise, right sides together. Using a ⅜-inch (1-cm) seam allowance, machine stitch the short edges together. Press the seam open.

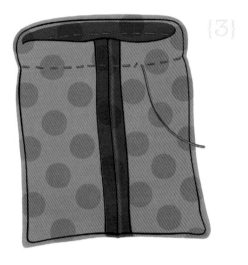

{3} With your machine set on the longest stitch setting possible, sew basting stitches along one of the long edges, securing your thread at only one end and leaving a long length of thread free at the other end.

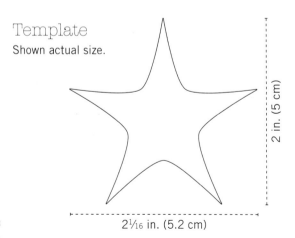

{4} Pull on the free end of thread to gather the lower edge and machine stitch through the gathers a few times to secure firmly. Your fabric will now have formed a cup shape. Turn the piece right side out.

## Template
Shown actual size.

2 in. (5 cm)

2¹⁄₁₆ in. (5.2 cm)

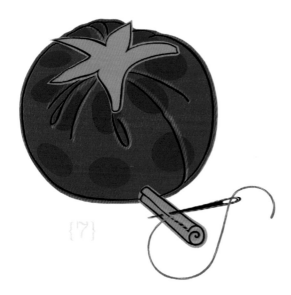

{5} Place a handful of rice or lentils into the pincushion, if required, and then a handful of polyester fiber filling.

## Stuffing your pincushion

To keep your needles and pins in tip-top sharp condition, you may want to fill the top part of your pincushion with fine steel wool or emery sand (some people also swear by aquarium sand). A number of experienced sewers also recommend wool scraps to help the pins stay smooth.

{6} Using a doubled length of thread, work a line of running stitches by hand (see page 7) around the top edge of the pincushion, ⅜ inch (1 cm) from the raw edge. Pull up tightly, tuck the raw edge in, and sew through the gathered fabric a few times to secure.

{7} Hand stitch the leaf to the top of the tomato in the center. Roll the small rectangle of felt for the stem into a long, thin tube and overcast the edge in place (see page 7). Stitch the stem to the center of the leaf. If you want to, take your thread all the way through the base of your pincushion and back up again before securing. This helps give your pincushion a nice squashy look and will make it feel firmer.

# Apple bag

If you need a decent-size tote bag that is strong enough to hold books, papers, and everything else you need during a busy day, then this one will fit the bill. The outside pockets are deep enough to hold small items without any danger of them dropping out, too. This example is made from a soft gray wool flannel with some boldly printed quilting cotton fabric for the lining. Check that your chosen lining does not have a directional pattern, or it won't work with this design. For a more summery look, you could try a medium-weight denim instead of the flannel.

## You will need

- ✂ Two 15 x 27-inch (38 x 69-cm) pieces of pale gray wool flannel fabric
- ✂ Two 15 x 28-inch (38 x 71-cm) pieces of coordinating printed cotton fabric for lining
- ✂ 4 x 51 inches (10 x 130 cm) pale gray wool flannel fabric for strap
- ✂ Pale gray sewing thread
- ✂ Thread to match your patterned fabric (if necessary)
- ✂ One 1¼-inch (32-mm) brown button
- ✂ Lime green sewing thread to secure the button
- ✂ Basic sewing kit (see page 4)
- ✂ Fabric marking pen

## Finished size

Bag: 14 inches (36 cm) wide by
15½ inches (39 cm) tall
Strap: 45 inches (114 cm) from the top
of one side of the bag to the other

# How to make the apple bag

{1} Place the two pale gray rectangles right sides together and machine stitch down the two long sides, using a ⅜-inch seam (1-cm) allowance. Press the seams open. Repeat with the printed cotton rectangles. You will now have two tube shapes that are open at both ends.

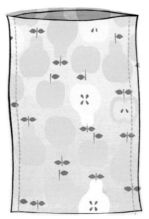

{1}

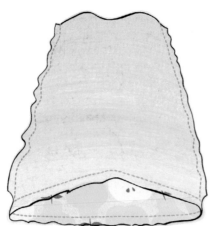

{2}

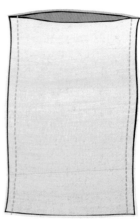

{2} Turn the patterned cotton tube right side out and insert it into the gray tube so that the side seams match and the raw edges along the tube openings meet at one end. Pin the tubes together around this opening, then machine stitch the pieces, using a ⅜-inch (1-cm) seam allowance.

{3} Turn the gray part right side out, so that you now have what looks like one long tube of fabric. Tuck the patterned fabric part of the tube into the gray part, so that the seam joining the two fabrics is on the inside of the doubled tube, ⅝ inch (1.5 cm) down from the folded edge. Machine stitch along the seam line where the two fabrics meet to secure the pieces in position. This will be the top edge of your bag.

{3}

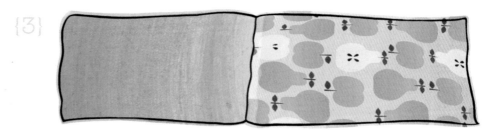

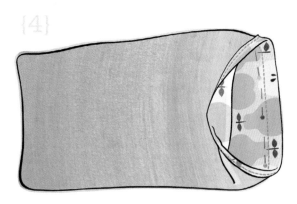

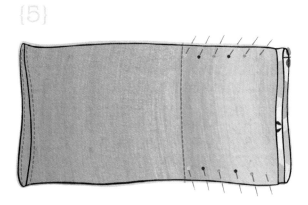

{4} At the opposite end of the tube, fold the patterned fabric under by ⅝ inch (1.5 cm) and press. Fold the fabric under by another ⅝ inch (1.5 cm) and press again. Place the folded edge over the gray fabric so that the raw edge of the gray fabric touches the inside of the fold of the patterned fabric, and pin in place. Machine stitch along the edge of the patterned fabric in matching thread. This edge will form the top edge of the pockets on the finished bag.

{5} Pin the side seams of the two tubes together for about 8 inches (20 cm), from the pocket edge upward (this keeps the fabric in place for the next stage). Measure 9½ inches (24 cm) up from the finished pocket edge at both sides of the tube. Using the fabric marking pen, draw a straight line across the bag between these two marks, then machine stitch across the line. Remove the straight pins from the side seams.

{6} Fold the pocket edge part of the bag upward all the way around the bag, so that the line you have just sewn forms the bottom of the bag and the pockets begin to take shape. Press lightly and pin the pocket part to the main part of the bag at the sides. On one side of the bag, using the fabric marking pen, draw two vertical lines on the pocket part, each one 4¾ inches (12 cm) from each side seam. On the other side of the bag, draw one vertical line in the center of the pocket piece. Pin along these lines through four layers of fabric to keep your fabric smooth for the next stage (not into all eight layers). Then machine stitch along all the lines to form the pocket dividers.

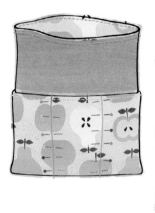

{7} At both bag side seams, machine stitch a short line of stitching from the top edge of the pocket part to the horizontal line of stitching around the pocket edge. (This will make sure the pockets look neat and stay in position.)

{8} Fold the gray strip that will form the bag strap in half lengthwise so that the right sides are together. Machine stitch along the long raw edges, using a ⅜-inch (1-cm) seam allowance. Turn up ⅝ inch (1.5 cm) along the two short edges and press. Turn the tube right side out through one of the short ends and press so that the seam lies on the inside, along one of the long edges.

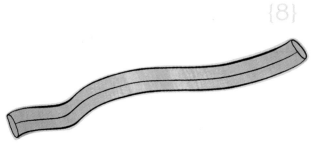

{9} Machine stitch around all four edges of the strap, ¼ inch (6 mm) in from the outside edge.

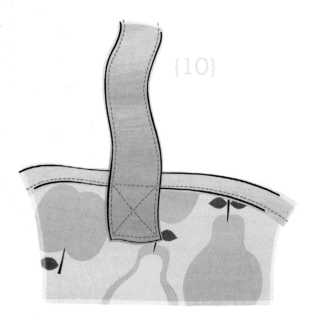

{10} Pin the strap to the sides of the bag on the inside, so that the strap lies over the side seams and the short edge of the strap lies 3 inches (7.5 cm) down from the top edge of the bag. Box stitch the strap to the bag, working the top edge of the box over the stitches around the top edge of the bag and the lower edge over the topstitch on the strap.

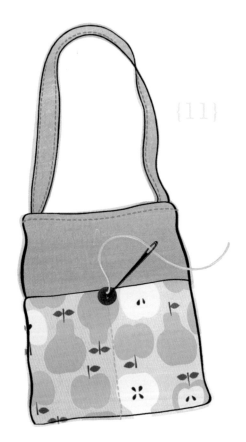

{11} Using contrasting lime green thread, sew the button in place at the top of the stitching that separates the two pockets on one side of the bag.

# Stash box

Any enthusiastic maker needs a stash box, or several, to keep all their essential odds and ends organized, whether it be knitting yarns, scraps of fabric, or crucial ribbons and trimmings. At 8 inches (20 cm) tall, the box shown here is roomy—but you can easily alter the dimensions of your pieces to create a complete stash storage system, with a range of boxes in different sizes. The handles are optional.

# You will need

- ✂ 18 inches (46 cm) cotton fabric, 45 inches (114 cm) wide, for outer part
- ✂ 18 inches (46 cm) cotton fabric, 45 inches (114 cm) wide, for lining
- ✂ 18 inches (46 cm) heavyweight iron-on fusible interfacing, 36 inches (91 cm) wide
- ✂ One 30-inch (76-cm) square of cotton batting for interlining
- ✂ Sewing thread to match your fabrics
- ✂ Basic sewing kit (see page 4)

# How to make the stash box

{1} From your main fabric (such as the fabric for the outer part), cut out one 12-inch (30-cm) square for the bottom, four 8¾ x 12-inch (22 x 30-cm) rectangles for the sides, and two 3 x 7-inch (7.5 x 18-cm) rectangles for the handles. From the lining fabric, cut out a bottom and four sides, matching the sizes of the main fabric. From the iron-on interfacing, cut out a bottom, four sides, and two handle pieces, also matching the sizes of the main fabric.

{2} With right sides together and aligning the raw edges, place one of the main fabric side pieces on the bottom. (If your fabric has a directional pattern, like ours, make absolutely sure that you align the *lower* edge of your side piece to the bottom, otherwise the pattern on your finished box will be upside down.) Machine stitch together, using a ⅜-inch (1-cm) seam allowance and beginning and ending your seam ⅜ inch (1 cm) from the raw edges. Repeat on the opposite side. Press the seams open.

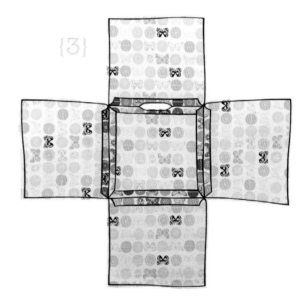

{3}

{3} Machine stitch the two other side pieces to the other sides of the bottom in the same way, leaving a 4-inch (10-cm) gap in the center of one side for turning the bag the right way out after you have sewn the lining in.

{4} Bring two adjacent side pieces right sides together so that the raw edges meet. Machine stitch them together, using a ⅜-inch (1-cm) seam allowance. Join the remaining sides in the same way.

{5} Iron the interfacing pieces to the reverse of your lining pieces. Machine stitch the lower edges of the side lining pieces to the bottom lining piece, as in steps 2 and 3—but do not leave a gap in one of the seams.

{6} Lay your lining piece face up on the cotton batting, pin in position, and sew all around the lining piece close to the edge. Trim away the excess batting. Complete the lining piece in the same way as in step 4.

{7} Iron the interfacing pieces for the handles onto the reverse of the main fabric pieces. Fold in ⅜ inch (1 cm) along the two long sides of both handle pieces and press. Then fold the two long sides together and press. Machine stitch close to the edge along the two long edges of the handle.

{8} Pin each handle in place at the top of the right side of the box, aligning the raw edges. The edges of the handles should be positioned 3¼ inches (8 cm) from the corner of the box. The long edge where the seam allowance has been folded in should be on the outside of the handle.

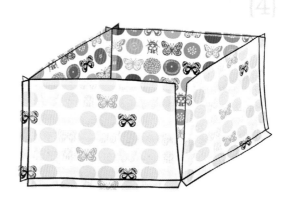

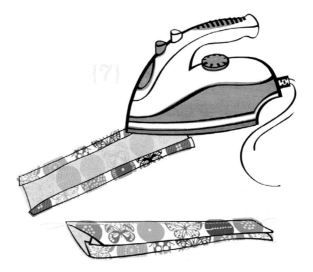

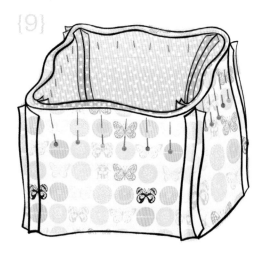

{9} With right sides together, matching the seams and aligning the top raw edges, place the lining in the outer box. Pin around the edges, then machine stitch around the top, using a ⅝-inch (1.5-cm) seam allowance, stitching back and forth over the handles to make sure they're really securely attached (see page 7).

{10} Turn the box right side out through the hole in the bottom of the outer piece. Slip-stitch the gap in the bottom closed (see page 7).

{11} Press the sides and bottom of the box, being particularly careful around the top edge so that the seam between the lining and outer fabric runs evenly along the top of the box. Topstitch around the top edge of the box, ⅜ inch (1 cm) down from the edge (see page 7).

# Valentine envelope

If you want to impress on Valentine's day, the wrapping is almost as important as the present. Fabric envelopes for small gifts are a fast-growing fashion and you can buy any number of designs in the stores—but it's much nicer to make something unique to reflect the thought behind your gift. The example here is 5 inches (13 cm) square—big enough to hold all kinds of treats, from candies to jewelry, yet still small enough to look cute. The size can easily be altered, however, to suit your own Valentine's offering.

## You will need

- ✂ Template on right
- ✂ Tracing paper and paper to make templates
- ✂ Pencil
- ✂ 9-inch (23-cm) square of printed cotton fabric for the outer part of the envelope
- ✂ 9-inch (23-cm) square of plain white linen fabric for the lining
- ✂ 9-inch (23-cm) square of fusible web
- ✂ 2¾ x 4-inch (7 x 10-cm) piece of bright pink felt and a matching piece of fusible web
- ✂ Snap fastener, ⅜ inch (1 cm) in diameter
- ✂ White round button, 1¹⁄₁₆ inch (18 mm) in diameter
- ✂ White heart-shape button, 1¹⁄₁₆ inch (18 mm) tall
- ✂ Thread to match your main fabric and felt
- ✂ Basic sewing kit (see page 4)
- ✂ Fabric marking pen

## Template

Shown at 33%; enlarge by 300% for actual size.

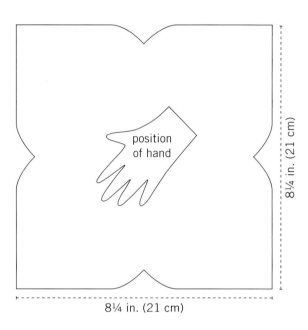

position of hand

8¼ in. (21 cm)

8¼ in. (21 cm)

# How to make the valentine envelope

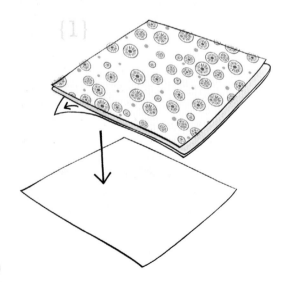

{1}

{1} Press the square of fusible web, glue side down, onto the reverse of your main fabric (see page 6). Peel the paper backing off the bonding web and press the main fabric down onto the reverse of your lining fabric.

{2} Prepare your envelope template, following the instructions on page 6, and cut it out. Lay the template on the lining side of your stiffened fabric. Draw around it with the fabric marking pen and cut it out.

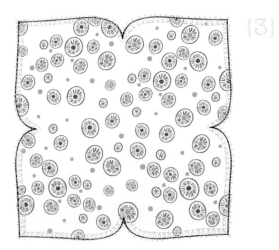

{3} Zigzag stitch around the entire shape, using your sewing machine.

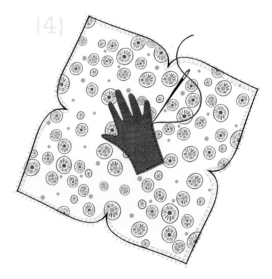

{4} Using the smaller piece of fusible web and the pink felt, prepare the appliqué motif (see page 6). Cut the appliqué motif out and apply it to the center of the envelope shape. Hand stitch around the edge of the hand in a small running stitch, using matching thread (see page 7).

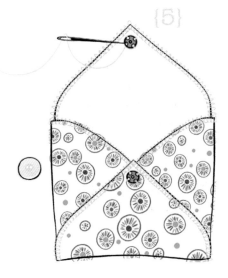

{5} Fold the sides of the envelope into the center and the lower edge upward, in line with the inner corners, and press. Secure in place by hand, working around the sides of the lower edge in a running stitch, along the inner edge of the zigzag stitching. Sew the top part of the snap fastener onto the wrong side of the top point of the envelope, about ⅜ inch (1 cm) down from the tip of the point. Sew the bottom of the snap fastener on the right side of the lower part of the envelope to correspond. Sew the round button in position on the right side of the top point of the envelope, so that it corresponds with the snap fastener.

{6} Finally, sew the heart-shape button in position in the center of the hand.

# Tablet case

Thick and soft, felt is available at every craft store or online supplier in a rainbow array of colors and at reasonable prices. Choose two favorite shades to create this custom-made case to keep your precious tablet safe from accidental bangs and scrapes. Although the case has got several layers, the making method is simple and doesn't involve any complicated turning. And once you've completed it, you can follow the same steps to create a matching case for your e-reader or any other slim gadget.

## You will need

- ✂ 12 x 20-inch (31 x 51-cm) piece of purple felt
- ✂ 9 x 12-inch (23 x 31-cm) piece of gray felt
- ✂ 1½ x 3¼-inch (4 x 8-cm) scrap of pink felt
- ✂ 12 x 23-inch (31 x 59-cm) piece of cotton fabric
- ✂ Fusible web
- ✂ 12 x 23 inches (31 x 59 cm) thin (2-ounce/60-g) polyester batting
- ✂ Two white buttons, ¾ inch (18 mm) in diameter
- ✂ 2-foot (60-cm) length of olive green embroidery thread
- ✂ Thread to match the purple felt
- ✂ Cream thread
- ✂ Basic sewing kit (see page 4)
- ✂ Paper for the template
- ✂ Pencil
- ✂ Fabric marking pen

# How to make the tablet case

{1} To make your templates, draw around your tablet remembering to keep your pencil vertical. Add a ⅜-inch (1-cm) seam allowance all around and ignore any rounded corners. Cut out the template. Draw around the template on a second piece of paper and cut out another rectangle. With the template facing you so that it is wider than it is tall, fold one lower corner up to the top edge, then unfold. Do the same with the other corner and unfold again. The folds on your paper should now show two triangles, one slightly larger than the other. Cut out the larger of the triangles to form the second part of your template and discard the remains of the paper. Trim the point of the triangle where the two equal sides meet to round it off.

{2} Using your two-part template and fabric marking pen, cut out the following:
✂ One triangle and one house-shape piece from the purple felt (use the triangle and rectangle combined to make the house shape) and one rectangle from the gray felt.
✂ Two pieces of fusible web for both the house and the rectangle shape and a single piece of fusible web for the triangle shape.
✂ One rectangle and one house shape from batting and from the cotton lining fabric.

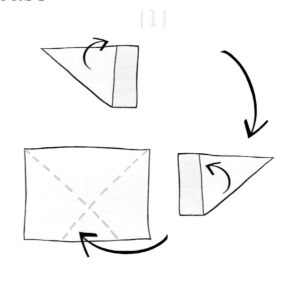

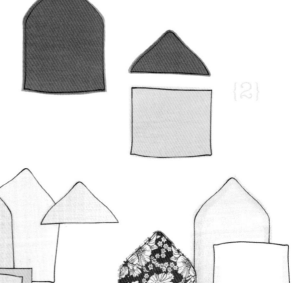

{3} Trim off ¼ inch (6 mm) around the entire edge of the two pieces of batting, so that they are exactly the same shape but slightly smaller than the felt pieces.

{4} Iron one of the house-shape pieces of fusible web, glue side down, onto the felt house shape (see page 6). Iron the other house-shape piece of fusible web onto the house-shape piece of lining fabric. Peel the backing paper off both pieces of fusible web. Sandwich the house-shaped batting between the felt and lining pieces and press in place. You will need to press the piece on both the lining side and the felt side and around the edges to make sure that your "sandwich" is secure.

{5} Repeat step 4 to make the rectangular part of your case.

{6} Apply the triangle of fusible web to the triangle of felt and press in place. Peel the backing paper off the triangle and press it onto the felt side of the rectangle. On your sewing machine, work straight stitch around the two equal sides of the triangle ³⁄₁₆ inch (5 mm) from the edge. Then zigzag stitch around these sides between the straight stitching and the raw edge of the triangle.

{7} On your sewing machine, straight stitch across the top of the rectangle, ⅜ inch (1 cm) from the edge. Trim the edge so that there is ³⁄₁₆ inch (5 mm) of fabric above the stitching. Zigzag stitch along the top of the rectangle between the straight stitching and the raw edge of the rectangle.

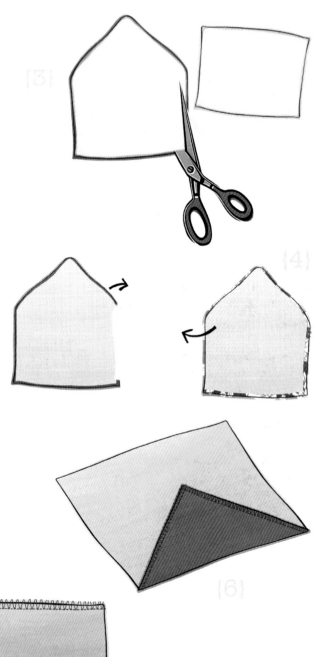

{8} With wrong sides together and the bottom of the triangle at the lower edge of the house-shape piece, place the rectangle on the house-shape piece. Pin the pieces in place. On your machine, straight stitch around the outer edge, including the pointed part of the house-shape piece, using a ⅜-inch (1-cm) seam allowance. Trim the seam allowance to ³⁄₁₆ inch (5 mm). Zigzag stitch around the outer edges of the entire piece between the straight stitches and raw edge.

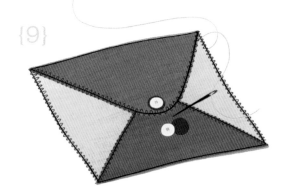

{9} Cut out two circles of pink felt, both slightly larger than your buttons (you can use a larger button as your template or any small round object of the right size). Place the felt circles under the buttons and, using cream thread, sew one button in place on the corner of the top flap and the other onto the main case, so that the felt circle comes just below the corner of the top flap when it is folded down.

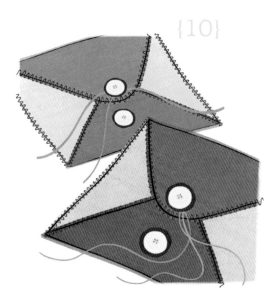

{10} Find the center of the length of embroidery thread and tie it around the top button, then divide the thread into three groups so there are four strands in each group. Braid the thread. When you are near the end, tie the three groups of thread together and trim the knot. Wrap the braided cord in a figure-eight around the two buttons to secure the case.

# Phone cozy

5–8 hrs

There are dozens of phone cases available in everything from leather to plastic, but you can easily create a good-looking, protective, and unique case for your cell phone, customized to your own taste. This pattern is fleece-lined to protect your phone, but the outer sleeve can be made from whatever fabric you prefer—plain or patterned, flat or textured. Our version has a small pocket—handy for headphones or bank or business cards—and it hooks shut with a simple button-and-elastic-loop device. The fleece lining has a slight gripping effect, making it less probable that your phone will slip out of its case accidentally.

## You will need

- Paper for template
- Pencil
- 8-inch (20-cm) square of plain heavyweight cotton or linen fabric
- 8-inch (20-cm) square of coordinating fleece for the lining
- 4 x 8-inch (10 x 20-cm) piece of printed cotton for the pocket
- 4-inch (10-cm) square of medium-weight iron-on fusible interfacing
- Threads to match your fabrics
- Thin hair elastic to match your plain fabric (or colored elastic cord)
- White button, ¾ inch (18 mm) in diameter
- Basic sewing kit (see page 4)
- Fabric marking pen

## How to make the phone cozy

{1} To prepare your main template, trace around your phone, being careful to hold your pencil at a right angle. Add ⅝ inch (1.5 cm) all around to allow for the seam allowance and the thickness of the phone, and ignore all rounded corners. Cut out the template.

{2} To prepare the pocket template, draw around your main template, then draw a line across the template at the halfway point. On the right-hand side, measure up 1 inch (2.5 cm) from the halfway line. Join this point to the halfway point on the left to form the top edge of the pocket. Cut out the template.

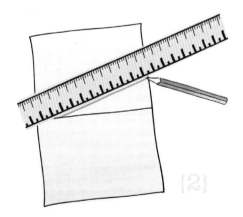

{2}

{3} Using the main template, cut out two pieces from your outer fabric and two pieces from the fleece. Trim the two fleece pieces so that they are ⅜ inch (1 cm) shorter and ¼ inch (6 mm) narrower than the outer pieces. Cut out two pocket pieces from your pocket fabric, one using the template the right way up and one using it face down. Cut one pocket piece from the interfacing. Cut out a rectangle of outer fabric measuring 1¾ x 2 inches (4.5 x 5 cm) for the tab.

{4} For the tab, fold the fabric under ¼ inch (6 mm) along both the long edges, then fold the piece in half lengthwise. Machine stitch close to the folded edges and press in half widthwise.

{5} Iron the interfacing onto the wrong side of one of the pocket pieces. Place the two pocket pieces right sides together and machine stitch along the sloping edge, using a ⅜-inch (1-cm) seam allowance. Turn right side out and press carefully, so that the seam runs along the center of the sloping edge. Topstitch ¼ inch (6 mm) down from the sloping edge (see page 7).

{6} Pin the pocket to the right side of one of the outer pieces, so that the pocket slopes upward from left to right. Pin the tab in place on top of the pocket piece, so that the bottom of the tab is 1⅛ inches (3 cm) up from the lower edge. The folded edge of the tab should face inward and the raw edges should line up with the raw edges of the main piece.

{7} Machine tack the elastic cord loop in place just to each side of the center on the right side of the second main piece (the piece without the pocket). Your tacking should be ⅜ inch (1 cm) from the raw edge and the loop should be about ⅝ inch (1.5 cm) long.

{8} Pin the two outer pieces right sides together and machine stitch around the sides and bottom, using a ⅜-inch (1-cm) seam allowance. Clip the corners (see page 7).

{9} Pin the two fleece pieces right sides together. Machine stitch around the sides and bottom, using a ⅜-inch (1-cm) seam allowance and leaving a 1½-inch (4-cm) gap in the center of the lower edge for turning. Trim the seam allowances and clip the corners. Turn the right way out.

{10} Place the fleece lining inside the outer part of the case (still wrong way out), making sure the pieces are right sides together and that the side seams match. Machine stitch around the top, using a ⅜-inch seam (1-cm) allowance, stitching back and forth over the elastic loop to make sure that it is really secure (see page 7).

{11} Turn the case right side out through the gap in the fleece lining, making sure that the pocket is on the correct side. Press the outer part of the case carefully and then, sewing by hand, slip-stitch the gap in the lining closed (see page 7). Push the lining down into the main case.

{12} Topstitch (see page 7) around the top of the case ¼ inch (6 mm) from the top edge. Sew the button in place, making sure it corresponds with the elastic loop.

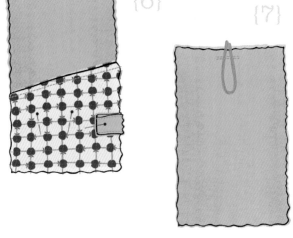

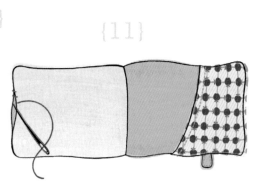

# Floor cushion

5-8 hrs

Floor cushions are a good answer to any temporary seating shortage, whether in a TV den or a teenager's bedroom. This one does double-duty as a storage container—it's cleverly stuffed with an extra bed comforter, which can be pulled out for an impromptu sleepover. The floor cushion needs to be made from an upholstery-weight fabric. The quantities in the materials list allow for using a directionally patterned fabric; if your choice is plain, or has a nondirectional pattern, such as a polka dot, you may need slightly less.

# You will need

- ✂ Templates on page 37
- ✂ Tracing paper and paper for templates
- ✂ Pencil
- ✂ 2½ yards (2.3 m) of fabric 43 inches (110 cm) wide or 1¾ yards (1.6 m) of fabric 59 inches (150 cm) wide
- ✂ Thread to match your fabric
- ✂ 18-inch (46-cm) closed-end general-purpose zipper to match your fabric
- ✂ Single bed comforter for stuffing
- ✂ Basic sewing kit (see page 4)
- ✂ Fabric marking pen
- ✂ Ruler
- ✂ Stitch ripper

# How to make the floor cushion

{1} Using the templates on page 37, cut out one top piece, two bottom pieces, and five side pieces. If your fabric is directional like ours, when cutting the bottom pieces, remember to cut one semicircle with the template the right way up and one semicircle with the template face down. You must also make sure that your pattern is the right way up on the side pieces, with the bottom of the pattern at the wider, lower end of the shape. For the handle, cut out a rectangle measuring 3¼ x 9 inches (8 x 23 cm).

{2} Use your sewing machine to zigzag stitch around all the pieces except for the handle.

{3} Pin the five side pieces right sides together and machine stitch, using a ⅝-inch (1.5-cm) seam allowance. Then stitch the first and fifth side pieces together, again using a ⅝-inch (1.5-cm) seam allowance. Press all the seams open.

{1}

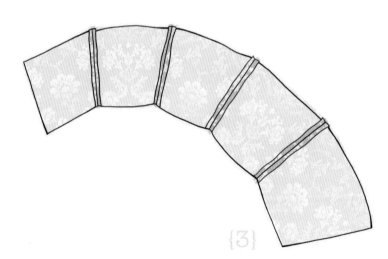

{3}

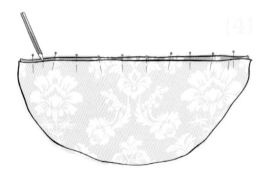

{4} Pin the two bottom pieces right sides together and measure 4½ inches (11 cm) in from each end of the straight edge. Mark these points with the fabric marking pen.

{5} Using a ⅝-inch (1.5-cm) seam allowance and a standard-length straight stitch, sew from one outer edge to the first mark, securing the stitching at the beginning and end by working a few stitches back and forth (see page 7). Change your machine to the longest stitch setting possible and sew to the second mark. Secure your thread by working a few stitches back and forth at the second mark and sew to the end using a standard-length straight stitch. Press the seam open.

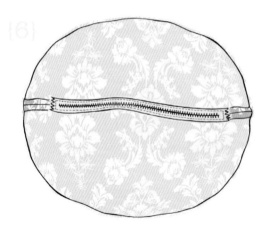

{6} Lay the zipper face down over the center part of the seam (where you have sewn the large stitches) on the wrong side of your work and pin in place. Machine stitch the zipper in place by working a thin rectangle all around it. You will need to move the zipper mechanism as you sew to make sure that your stitching is smooth.

{7} With the right side of your work facing, use your stitch ripper to undo the large stitches running down the center of the zipper, between the markers.

{8} Fold the handle piece in half lengthwise, right sides together, and machine stitch along the long edges, using a ⅜-inch (1-cm) seam allowance. Turn the handle right side out. Fold in ⅜ inch (1 cm) along each of the short edges and press the handle so that the long seam runs along the middle of the handle. Sew a line of stitching close to the edge around the entire handle.

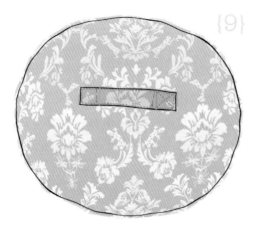

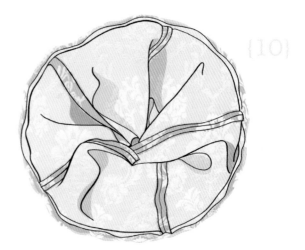

{9} Pin the handle right side up in the center of the top piece of the floor cushion. Measure up 1 inch (2.5 cm) from each end of the stitching on the short edges of the handle and, using the fabric marking pen, draw a line across the handle. Use these lines as a guide to secure the handle by machine stitching a square with a box stitch inside at each end.

{10} With right sides together, pin the sides to the bottom. Machine stitch, using a ⅝-inch (1.5-cm) seam allowance.

{11} Open the zipper in the bottom piece. With right sides together, pin the top to the sides. Machine stitch, using a ⅝-inch (1.5-cm) seam allowance.

{12} Turn the cushion cover right side out through the open zipper and press. Insert the comforter into the cover and close the zipper.

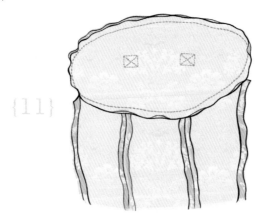

# Templates

Shown at 20%; enlarge by 500% for actual size.

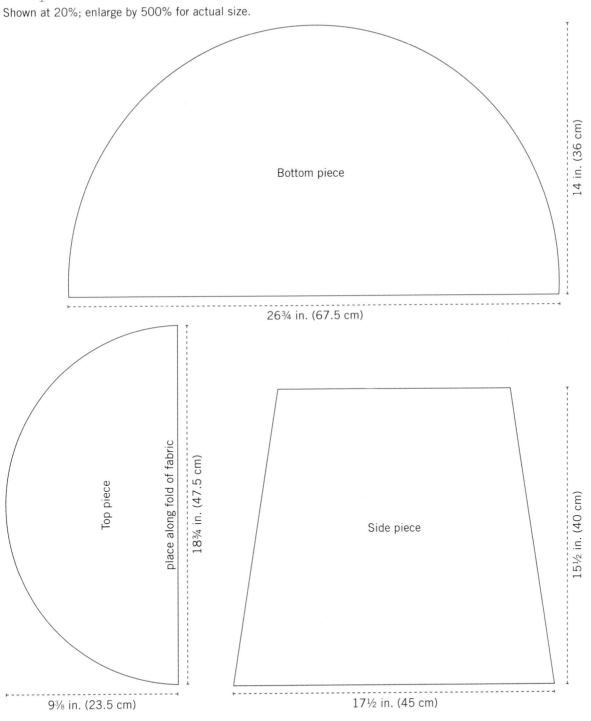

Bottom piece

14 in. (36 cm)

26¾ in. (67.5 cm)

Top piece

place along fold of fabric

18¾ in. (47.5 cm)

9⅜ in. (23.5 cm)

Side piece

15½ in. (40 cm)

17½ in. (45 cm)

# Doll-face pillows

9-12 hrs

This pair of pillows, inspired by a set of painted wooden Scandinavian dolls, is an ideal choice to liven up kids' bedrooms. The fronts are made from felt with appliquéd features and the backs are made from polyester fleece to give them a nice, soft feel. Once you've made one pair, you can invent a whole range of characters, changing the hair, eyes, and so on by varying the shapes and colors of the appliqués.

# You will need

*For each pillow*

&times; Templates on pages 43–44

&times; Pencil

&times; 21½ x 46-inch (55 x 117-cm) piece of pale pink felt

&times; 16 x 31½-inch (41 x 80-cm) piece of light mauve polyester fleece fabric

&times; Small piece of light pink polyester fleece or felt for the cheeks

&times; Small piece of black felt for the eyes

&times; 8-inch (20-cm) square of fusible web

&times; 15-inch (38-cm) circular pillow insert form

&times; Dark gray embroidery thread

&times; Light pink and mauve sewing threads

&times; Pair of compasses

&times; Basic sewing kit (see page 4)

*For the man pillow*

&times; 8 x 16-inch (20 x 41-cm) piece of dark brown flannel or felt

&times; Small piece of red felt for the mouth

&times; Dark brown and red sewing threads

*For the woman pillow*

&times; 12 x 16-inch (31 x 41-cm) gray flannel or felt

&times; Small piece of bright pink felt for the mouth

&times; Gray and bright pink sewing threads

# How to make the doll-face pillows

[1] To make the templates for the pillow front and the two pieces for each pillow back, use the pair of compasses and pencil to draw three circles, each 15 inches (38 cm) in diameter. Cut out one whole circle for each pillow front. For the back pieces, cut the circles as shown, remembering to straighten the sides of the lower edge of each inner back piece (this will help make sure the hem on this piece is neat).

[2] Use the front template to cut out the front of each pillow from pale pink felt. Also cut a strip of pale pink felt measuring 4 x 45 inches (10 x 115 cm) for the side strip of each pillow. Cut out the two back pieces for each pillow from the fleece fabric.

[3] Using the templates on pages 43–44, cut out the hairpieces from dark brown flannel or felt for the man's hair and gray flannel or felt for the woman's hair.

[4] Trace the templates from pages 43–44 for two sets of facial features—the eyes, nose, cheeks, and mouth—and the mustache for the man onto the backing paper of the piece of fusible web. Cut out the shapes on the fusible web coarsely, not too close to the pencil outlines. Iron the fusible web onto the reverse side of the appropriate fabrics (check the photo on pages 38–39), remembering to have your iron on a fairly low setting (see page 6).

[5] Peel the backing paper off the face appliqués and position them on the fronts of the pillows, using the photographs as a guide. Use the hairpieces to help you position the features, but do not attach them just yet. Once you are happy with their positions, iron the facial features in place, again remembering to have your iron on a fairly low setting.

[6] Work hand running stitching (see page 7) around the noses, using light pink thread. For the man, work running stitching around the edge of the mouth, using red sewing thread. For the woman, overcast the mouth in place around the inner and outer circles, using bright pink sewing thread (see page 7). On both pillows, machine stitch around the cheeks, just in from the edges, using zigzag stitching and light pink thread. By hand, using two strands of dark gray embroidery thread, sew six straight stitches out from the center of the eye to just over the edge— the stitches should form a star shape over the eye. For the woman, use three strands of dark gray embroidery thread to work three straight stitches above each eye for eyelashes. For the man, machine stitch around the mustache, using zigzag stitching and brown sewing thread.

[7] Pin the hairpieces in position and machine stitch them in place with zigzag stitching only along the inside parts, using matching thread.

[8] Fold each side strip in half widthwise. Using matching thread and a ⅜-inch (1-cm) seam allowance, machine stitch the two short edges together. The side strips will now be a circle. Press the seam open.

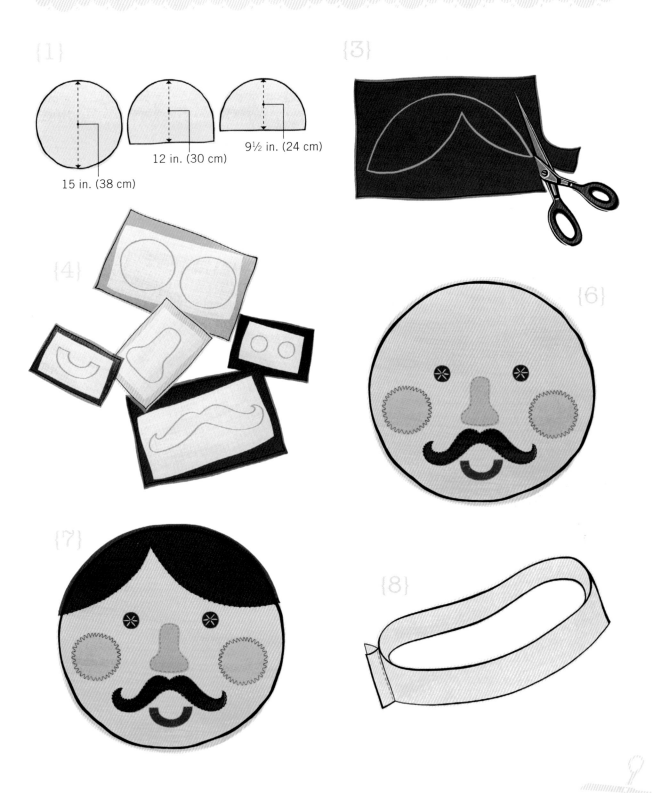

{1}

15 in. (38 cm)

12 in. (30 cm)

9½ in. (24 cm)

{3}

{4}

{6}

{7}

{8}

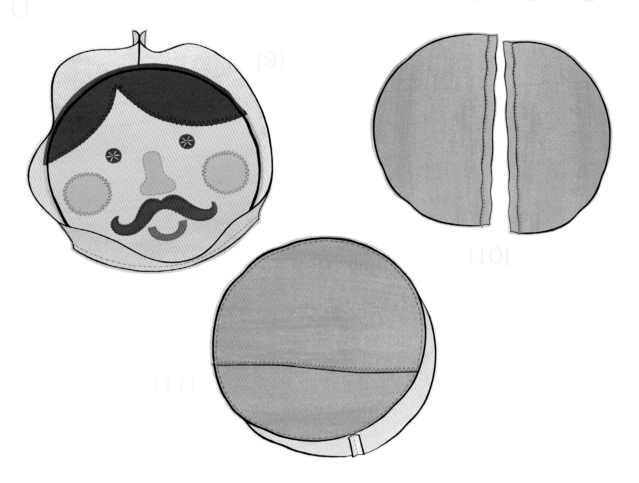

{9} With right sides together, pin one long edge of a side strip around the outer edge of the front of each pillow, placing the seam of the side strip at the top of the head. Using light pink thread and a ⅜-inch (1-cm) seam allowance, machine stitch the strips in place.

{10} Fold under 1⅛ inches (3 cm) along the straight edges of one of the back pieces. Pin it in position, then work a machine zigzag stitch along the raw edge to secure the edge in place. Repeat for the other back piece.

{11} With right sides together, pin the outer back piece of each pillow (the smaller piece) to the side strip, so that the straight edge of the back piece goes across the center of the face, from one side to the other. Now pin the inner back piece (the larger piece) right side down to the side strip, so that its straight edge overlaps the straight edge of the other outer piece. Using light pink thread and a ⅜-inch (1-cm) seam allowance, machine stitch the back pieces to the side piece by sewing around the entire outside edge.

{12} Turn the pillow covers right side out and insert the pillow forms.

## Templates

Shown at 40%; enlarge by 250% for actual size.

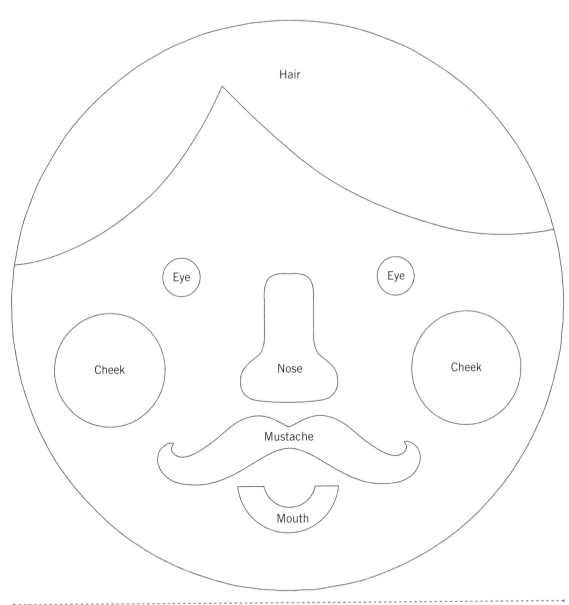

15 in. (38 cm) diameter

## Templates
Shown at 40%; enlarge by 250% for actual size.

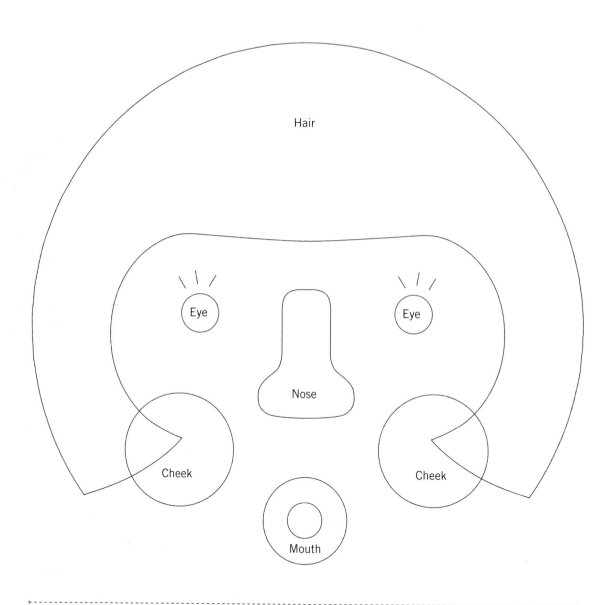

15 in. (38 cm) diameter

# Sensory play mat

Help the baby in your life begin to get accustomed to all the textures and sounds surrounding them with a homemade play mat that offers a range of different sensations. The petals are made from an assortment of fabrics, including toweling, velour, cotton honeycomb (or waffle cloth), and fleece—so each petal looks or feels different. Crinkly cellophane, bells, and a squeaker were sewn inside separate petals for some added fun for the baby to explore. The play mat measures about 56 inches (142 cm) across. With supervision, the mat is suitable for babies from birth to around 15 months.

## You will need

- ✂ Template on page 47
- ✂ Paper for template
- ✂ 43-inch (110-cm) square of fabric for the flower center
- ✂ 43-inch (110-cm) square of fleece fabric for the backing
- ✂ 43-inch (110-cm) square of 4-ounce (125-g) polyester batting
- ✂ Eight assorted fabrics measuring approximately 16 x 24 inches (41 x 61 cm) for each of the eight petals; I used four plain-colored textured fabrics and four coordinating printed cottons
- ✂ Sewing thread to match your fabrics
- ✂ 10 ounces (280 g) polyester fiber filling
- ✂ Squeaker, bells, and crinkly cellophane
- ✂ 30-inch (76-cm) length of string
- ✂ Fabric marking pen and quilter's pencil
- ✂ Ruler
- ✂ Long quilter's safety pins
- ✂ Basic sewing kit (see page 4)

## How to make the play mat

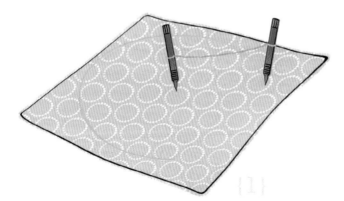

{1} To draw the large octagon for the main section of the play mat, tie one end of your string around the fabric marking pen and the other around the quilter's pencil. The length of string between the pen and pencil should be about 20 inches (51 cm). Lay out your flower center fabric on a large surface or the floor. Holding the quilter's pencil at the center of your fabric and keeping the string taut, move the fabric marking pen completely around the pencil to draw a large circle. Cut out the circle.

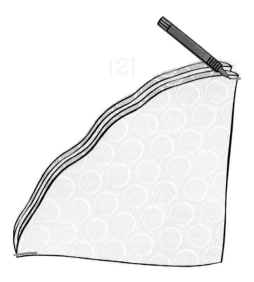

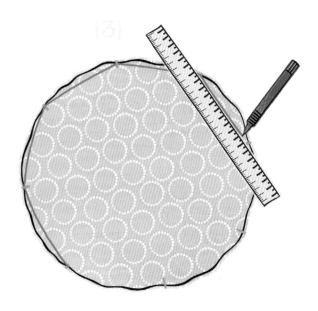

{2} Fold the flower center piece of fabric in quarters and mark each quarter at the edge. Fold each quarter in half and mark the center points. You should now have eight marks around the edge of your fabric.

{3} Draw a straight line from one mark to the next all around the fabric edge and cut along these lines to make an octagon. Lay the flower center on top of your backing fabric and use it as a template to cut out another octagon. Cut out an octagon of batting in the same way.

{4} Use the template, see right, to make the petals. If you want to make sure the size at the bottom edge of the petal matches the section of the octagonal flower center it will be attached to, measure across the octagonal section, ⅜ inch (1 cm) from the outer edge, then add ¾ inch (2 cm) to this measurement. This will give you the correct measurement for the bottom edge of the petal for that particular section.

## Template
Shown at 20%; enlarge by 500% for actual size. To make sure the curves are even, fold paper in half along a vertical line in the center.

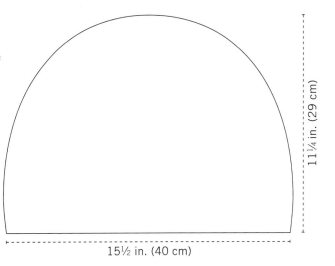

11¼ in. (29 cm)

15½ in. (40 cm)

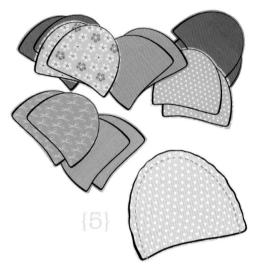

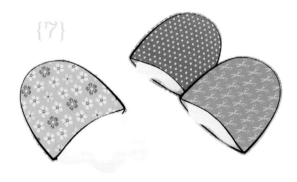

{5} For each of the eight petals, fold each piece of fabric in half, pin the template on top, and cut out two petal pieces in the same fabric. Place the two pieces right sides together and machine stitch around the curved edge, using a ⅜-inch (1-cm) seam allowance.

{7} Stuff all the petals lightly and evenly with polyester fiber filling; each flower petal should be 1–1½ inches (2.5–4 cm) thick. Insert the squeaker, bells, and crinkly cellophane into the chosen petals; I put them into the petals made from printed cottons instead of the ones made from textured fabric. If necessary, wrap the squeaker and bells in scraps of batting before you put them into the petals to help them stay in place.

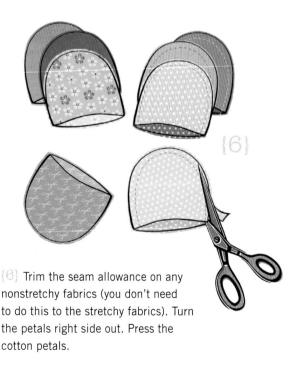

{6} Trim the seam allowance on any nonstretchy fabrics (you don't need to do this to the stretchy fabrics). Turn the petals right side out. Press the cotton petals.

{8} Place the petals face down on the right side of the flower center so that the straight edge of each petal lines up with one side of the flower center octagon. Pin, then tack the petals in position by hand, ⅜ inch (1 cm) from the raw edges.

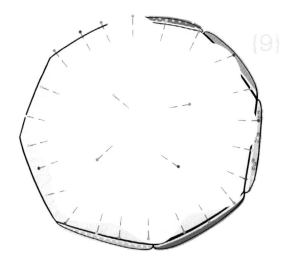

{9} Place the backing fabric octagon right side down on the flower center, carefully aligning all the edges, then place the batting on top. Pin in place, working from the center outward, making sure you use plenty of long quilter's pins across the middle of the piece as well as around the edges.

{10} Turn the flower over, so that the wrong side of the main flower center is facing upward. Using a ⅜-inch (1-cm) seam allowance, machine stitch around the edge of the flower center, removing the pins from underneath as you sew and leaving a 10-inch (25.5-cm) gap in the center of one of the petals for turning. (You will find it easiest if you leave the gap in one of the cotton fabric petals instead of in one of the petals made from thick or stretchy fabric.)

{11} Turn the play mat right side out through the gap. Press the edges of the gap under, in line with the seam, on both the back and the front of the play mat and pin in position. Slip-stitch the gap closed by hand (see page 7).

{12} Press the flower center and the cotton petals lightly, being especially careful not to iron any synthetic fabrics you have used for your play mat, such as synthetic velour fabric.

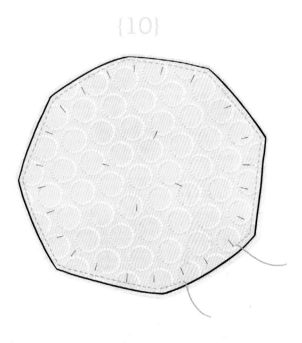

## Check your fabrics

When making the play mat, it is very important to wash all the fabrics before you use them, and to double check that they are all colorfast and nontoxic because babies may put them in their mouths.

# Toy boat

This is one of the simplest toys you could ever sew. The secret to making it look wonderful lies in your fabric choices. Our version used a plain color for the hull, with two patterns for the sails and some coordinating ribbon. The boat is 12 inches (30 cm) tall. You can easily alter the template to make your own boat bigger or smaller—but remember that you might need wider or narrower ribbon for the flags if you do this.

## You will need

✂ Two pieces of patterned fabric for the sails, each measuring 12 x 14 inches (31 x 36 cm)

✂ 5 x 12-inch (13 x 31-cm) piece of plain fabric for the hull

✂ 6-inch (15 cm) length of red ribbon, ⅝ inch (15 mm) wide

✂ Sewing threads to match the fabrics

✂ 1½ ounces (45 g) polyester fiber filling

✂ One toy rattle insert

✂ Templates on page 54

✂ Pencil and paper

✂ Basic sewing kit (see page 4)

## Make it personal

For a fun addition to the boat, why not embroider the name of the recipient on the hull—and perhaps add his or her age on the right-hand sail?

# How to make the toy boat

[1] Using the templates on page 54, cut out two sail pieces from the first sail fabric and two sail pieces from the second sail fabric, remembering to cut one piece of each fabric with the template the right way up and the other piece with the template face down. Cut out two hull pieces from the plain fabric. Cut the ribbon into three 2-inch (5-cm) lengths.

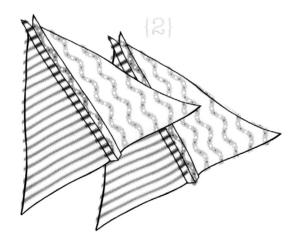

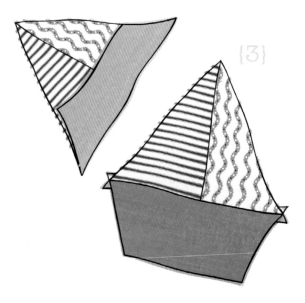

[2] Place two sail pieces, one of each fabric, right sides together. Using a ⅜-inch (1-cm) seam allowance, machine stitch them together down the side that forms a right angle to the short edge. Repeat with the remaining two sail pieces. Press the seams open.

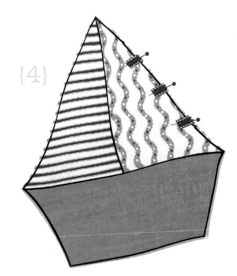

[3] With right sides together, aligning the long edge of the hull with the bottom of the sail, pin one hull piece to one of the double sail pieces. Using a ⅜-inch (1-cm) seam allowance, machine stitch them together. Press the seam open. Do the same with the other sail and hull piece.

[4] Fold each piece of ribbon in half. Pin the ribbon loops along one side of the sail at 2-inch (5-cm) intervals so that the raw edges of the ribbon line up with the raw edges of the fabric and the loops point inward.

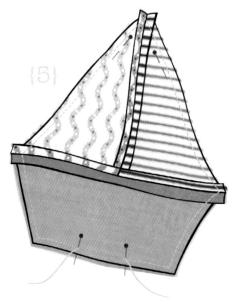

{5} With right sides together, pin the two boat pieces together, making sure that the seams match. Using a ⅜-inch (1-cm) seam allowance, machine stitch around the shape, using matching threads, changing color where necessary and leaving a 3½-inch (9-cm) gap along the lower edge of the hull for turning and stuffing.

{6} Snip off the corners of the hull and the point at the top of the sails, being careful not to cut into the stitching. Turn the boat right side out through the gap and press the seams flat.

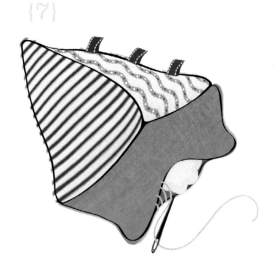

{7} Stuff the boat lightly, inserting the rattle into the sail part of the boat. Slip-stitch the gap at the lower edge of the hull closed by hand (see page 7).

{8} Work a few hand stitches, one over the other, through both layers of the boat at the point where the lower edges of the sails meet at the center of the hull to pull it in and create the boat shape.

# Templates

Shown at 50%; enlarge by 200% for actual size.

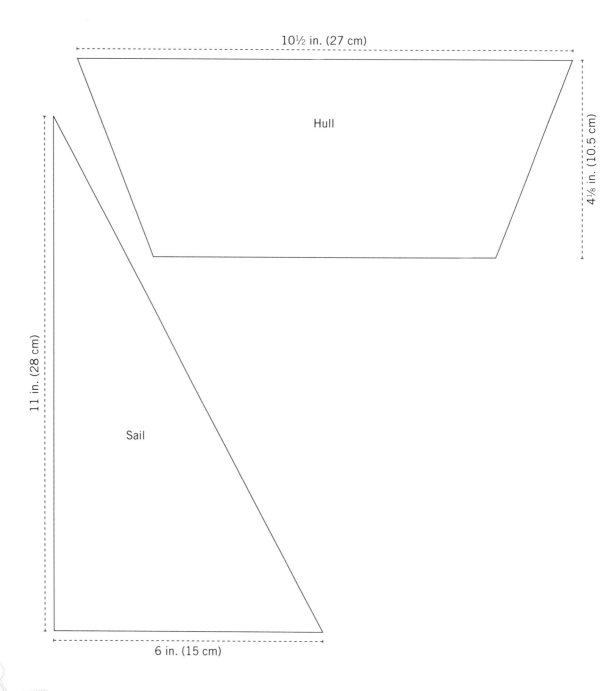

10½ in. (27 cm)

Hull

4⅛ in. (10.5 cm)

11 in. (28 cm)

Sail

6 in. (15 cm)

# Antarctic play set

Small enough for little hands, and engaging enough to spark any junior imagination, this penguin play set is bound to become a favorite. With a helping hand, the penguins can nestle in their icy cave, dive into the pond to chase for fish … or just generally waddle about. The whole miniature scenario makes a good travel toy, too, because it's light and little enough to carry around and balance on a car or bus seat. Each penguin is about 2½ inches (6 cm) high.

# You will need

## For each penguin

- ✂ Templates below
- ✂ Pencil and paper
- ✂ 3 x 5½-inch (7.5 x 14-cm) piece of black or dark gray felt
- ✂ 1½ x 2½-inch (4 x 6-cm) piece of white felt
- ✂ Scrap of orange felt
- ✂ White and black sewing threads
- ✂ Short length of black embroidery thread
- ✂ Small handful of polyester fiber filling
- ✂ PVA or white craft glue

## For the icy landscape

- ✂ Two 9 x 13-inch (23 x 33-cm) pieces of white felt
- ✂ 3½ x 4½-inch (9 x 11.5-cm) piece of mid-blue felt
- ✂ White and blue sewing threads

## For the fish

- ✂ 2 x 3-inch (5 x 7.5-cm) piece of green felt
- ✂ Green sewing thread
- ✂ Short length of black embroidery thread
- ✂ Fabric marking pen
- ✂ Basic sewing kit (see page 4)

## Templates
Shown at actual size.

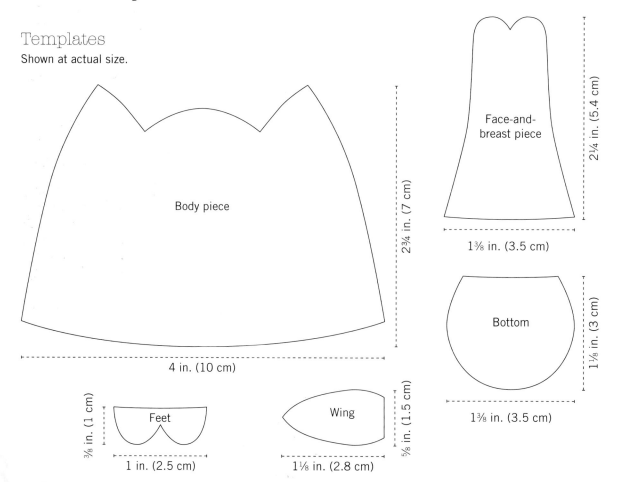

Body piece

2¾ in. (7 cm)

4 in. (10 cm)

Face-and-breast piece

2¼ in. (5.4 cm)

1⅜ in. (3.5 cm)

Bottom

1⅛ in. (3 cm)

1⅜ in. (3.5 cm)

Feet

⅜ in. (1 cm)

1 in. (2.5 cm)

Wing

⅝ in. (1.5 cm)

1⅛ in. (2.8 cm)

# How to make the penguins

[1] Using the templates on page 56, cut out one body piece, two wings, and a bottom from black or gray felt, one face-and-breast piece from white felt, and one foot piece from orange felt.

[2] Place the face-and-breast piece on the center of the body piece, then work a small running stitch, using white thread, to sew it in position (see page 7).

[3] Fold the body piece in half so that the face-and-breast piece is on the inside. Using black thread, overcast the back seam. Press the front and back of the head piece together and overcast the top seam.

[4] Turn the penguin right side out. Overcast the tops of the wings in place on the penguin's sides (see page 7).

[5] Embroider two French knots (see the box on page 58) for the eyes, using two strands of black embroidery thread.

[6] Stuff the penguin with polyester fiber filling. Overcast the bottom in place, beginning at the edge of the bottom of the face-and-breast piece and working around the back of the penguin first. Tuck the foot piece in position at the front and continue overcasting stitches across the bottom of the face-and-breast piece, catching the foot piece as you sew.

[7] Cut out a tiny triangle of orange felt for the beak and glue it in place.

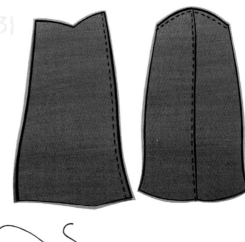

## fish

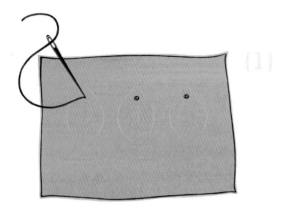

{1} Using the fabric marking pen, draw some small fish shapes on the green felt—but do not cut them out just yet. Using two strands of black embroidery thread, work a French knot on each fish for the eyes.

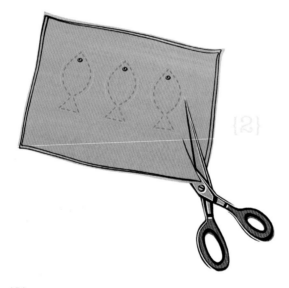

{2} Place the felt with the fish shapes on top of another piece of green felt, and machine stitch around the fish shapes. Cut out the fish shapes, cutting close to the stitching.

## icy landscape

{1} Stack the two pieces of white felt together and use the fabric marking pen to draw simple rounded corners at the two corners on one of the short ends of both rectangles of white felt. Cut along the lines to round off the corners.

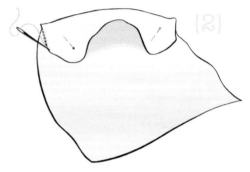

{2} Bring the rounded corners of one rectangle toward you, pushing them in toward each other as you do so, to form a small arch about 3 inches (7.5 cm) high, then pin the corners in place approximately halfway down the length of the piece of felt. Overcast along one lower side of the cave, using small stitches. Where the edge lifts to form the arch, secure the thread, then work a small running stitch around the edge of the arch (see page 7). When the arch stops, secure the thread, then overcast along the second side of the cave. Remove the pins.

## How to make a French knot

Bring your thread out at your starting point. Wind the thread twice around your needle, then take the needle into your fabric just to the side of the starting point. Pull the needle through your fabric, sliding the knot off your needle and onto the fabric as you pull.

{4} Work a machine zigzag stitch around the sides and back of the rectangle, then work a curved line of zigzag stitch across the front, following the line just drawn. Now, work a line of machine straight stitch along the inside edge of all the zigzag stitching. Trim across the front, just in front of your stitching, being careful not to cut into the stitches.

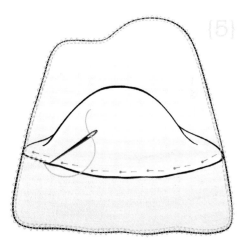

{5} Flatten the arch temporarily and pin it in place. Overcast the back of the cave to the bottom rectangle of felt, using small stitches.

{6} For the pond, cut out an oval shape measuring about 3 x 4 inches (7.5 x 10 cm) from the piece of mid-blue felt. Pin the pond in place. Zigzag stitch around the outside of the pond in matching thread, then switch your machine to straight stitch to sew along the inside edge of the zigzag stitch.

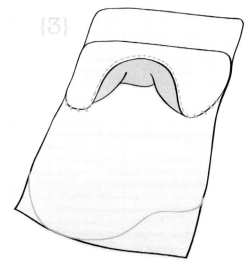

{3} Place the rectangle with the arch on top of the other rectangle of white felt, so that the front edges meet, and pin them together. Using the fabric marking pen, draw a curved line toward the front of the rectangle. The line does not have to be identical to the one shown, but remember to curve the edges inward at the sides.

# Skinny-ear rabbit

If you want to make a relaxed companion for gentle playtime, check out this Scandinavian-style bunny. The mix of square body and long, thin ears made it the standout favorite with the smaller children who played with it—the ears were perfect for chewing and the body for hugging! The plain linen in our version seems to give it a touch of "heirloom quality," but you can make it in most medium-weight cotton fabrics of your choice. The rabbit is about 11 inches (28 cm) high. If you make it for a child under 36 months, please omit the button.

## You will need

- ✂ Templates on page 63
- ✂ Pencil
- ✂ Paper
- ✂ 8 x 14-inch (20 x 36-cm) piece of white linen
- ✂ 6½ x 15-inch (16.5 x 38-cm) piece of printed quilting cotton
- ✂ Dark gray stranded embroidery thread
- ✂ Red and white sewing threads
- ✂ 12-inch (31-cm) length of red rickrack trim
- ✂ ⅝-inch (15-mm) blue button (optional)
- ✂ 1½ ounces (43 g) polyester fabric filling
- ✂ Fabric marking pen
- ✂ Basic sewing kit (see page 4)

# How to make the skinny-ear rabbit

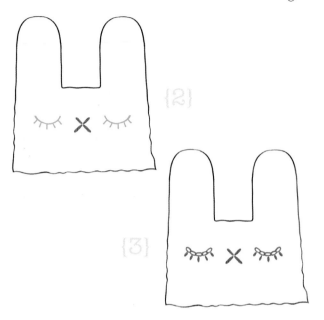

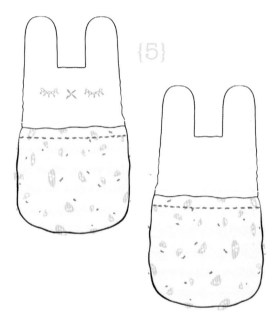

{1} Using the templates on page 63, cut out two head pieces from the white linen and two body pieces from the printed cotton.

{2} Using the template and the photo on page 60 as a guide, draw the two eyes and the nose on one of the head pieces, using the fabric marking pen. Using all six strands of the gray embroidery thread, hand sew four straight stitches in an X shape for the nose.

{3} Using three strands of dark gray embroidery thread, sew the main part of the eyes by hand in chain stitch (see box). Using the same thread, work the eyelashes in straight stitch.

{4} Pin the rickrack trim in position 1 inch (2.5 cm) down from the top raw edge of the body piece. Machine stitch it in place down the center of the trim, using red thread.

{5} Place the two head pieces on the two body pieces, with right sides together and aligning the straight edges. Using white thread and a ⅜-inch (1-cm) seam allowance, machine stitch the pieces together along the straight edges. Press the seam toward the body part of the two rabbit shapes.

## How to work chain stitch

Bring your needle out at your starting point. Take the needle back into your fabric, just next to the starting point to create a small loop of thread. Bring the needle back up through your fabric a stitch length along and catch the loop with the needle. Pull your thread up gently through the loop until the stitch is firm.

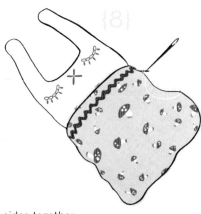

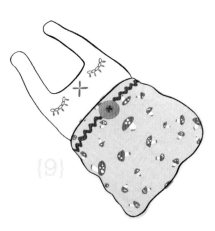

{6} Pin the two rabbit shapes right sides together. Using a ⅜-inch (1-cm) seam allowance, machine stitch around the outside of the shapes, leaving a 2½-inch (6-cm) gap along one side for turning and stuffing.

{7} Snip into the corners of the rabbit shape at the inner ears, being careful not to cut into the stitching. Turn the rabbit right side out through the gap and press flat.

{8} Stuff the rabbit firmly, using the blunt end of a pencil to push the fiber filling up to the tips of the ears. Slip-stitch the gap at the side closed by hand (see page 7).

{9} Using red thread, sew the button in place at the center of the rickrack trim on the front of the rabbit.

## Templates
Shown at 40%; enlarge by 250% for actual size.

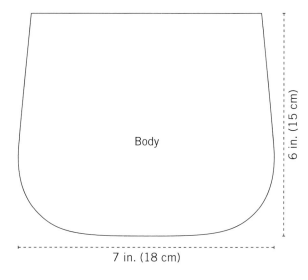

Body

6 in. (15 cm)

7 in. (18 cm)

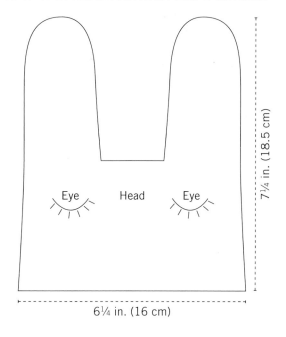

Eye     Head     Eye

7¼ in. (18.5 cm)

6¼ in. (16 cm)

# Fabric garland

If your offcuts stash is starting to run over with teeny pieces of gorgeous fabrics, these garlands are a terrific way to use them. These days, fabric garlands aren't reserved for special celebrations—they're a regular ornamental addition to interior decor and look great in children's bedrooms. We made ours in three contrasting cottons, but you could make every flag different if you want a more eclectic feel. And to make a longer garland, just increase the length of the ribbon and measure how many extra shapes it will take to fill it.

# You will need

*For a 2-yard (2-m) garland*

✂ Template on page 67

✂ Tracing paper and paper for template

✂ Pencil

✂ Three cotton quilting fabrics in the following sizes:
9½ x 14 inches (24 x 36 cm) for the thin rectangle garland pieces (fabric A)
12½ x 16½ inches (32 x 42 cm) for the wide rectangle garland pieces (fabric B)
17½ x 21 inches (45 x 54 cm) for the curved garland pieces (fabric C)

✂ Thread to match your fabrics

✂ 2-yard (2-m) coordinating narrow ribbon

✂ Selection of buttons, lace, and embroidery threads

✂ Basic sewing kit (see page 4)

✂ Fabric marking pen

✂ Embroidery needle

✂ Large-eye blunt sewing needle

# How to make the fabric garland

{1} Make templates for the three basic garland shapes. Use the template on page 67 for the curved shape and make your own templates for the rectangles: the thin rectangle pieces measure 3¼ x 7 inches (8 x 18 cm) and the wide rectangles measure 5½ x 6¼ inches (14 x 16 cm). The featured garland consists of four thin rectangles and three each of the other two shapes. Each "flag" needs two pieces of fabric—so cut out eight thin rectangle shapes from fabric A, six wide rectangles from fabric B, and six curved shapes from fabric C.

{2} Pin two of each shape right sides together. On one of the pieces of each "flag," measure ⅜ inch (1 cm) and 1 inch (2.5 cm) down from the top raw edge and mark these points on each side with a fabric marking pen—these mark where to leave gaps for the ribbon.

{3} Using a ⅜-inch (1-cm) seam allowance, machine stitch around the edges of each flag, leaving the top edge and the gaps between the two marks open, securing your thread each time you start and stop stitching (see page 7). Clip the curves on the curved flags and clip the lower corners of the rectangles (see page 7).

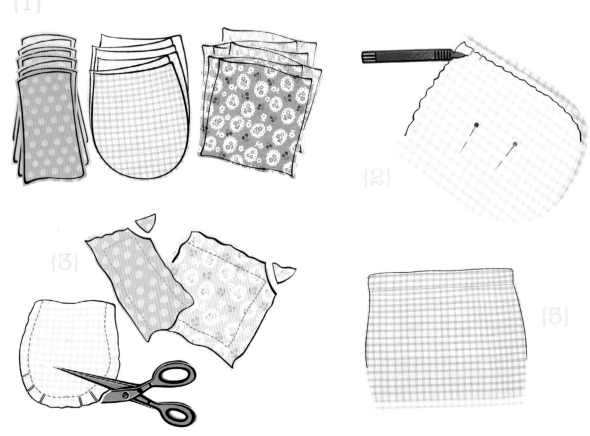

{4} Turn all the pieces right side out and press.

{5} Fold in ⅜ inch (1 cm) at the top raw edge of each piece and press. Machine stitch across the top of the flag close to the folded edge, then sew another line of stitching across the flag ⅝ inch (1.5 cm) down from the folded edge to form the casing for the ribbon.

{6} Decorate the pieces using lace, buttons, and embroidery thread as shown in the main photograph, stitching through both layers of fabric. The choice of embellishment is yours.

{7} Beginning and ending with a narrow rectangle, arrange the "flags" in order. Using the large-eye blunt needle, thread the narrow ribbon through the casing at the top of each piece of flag.

## Template

Shown at 50%; enlarge by 200% for actual size.

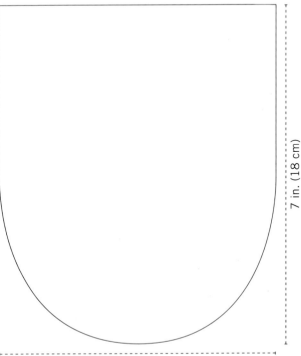

7 in. (18 cm)

6 in. (15 cm)

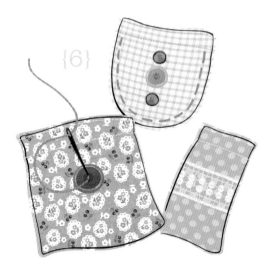

{6}

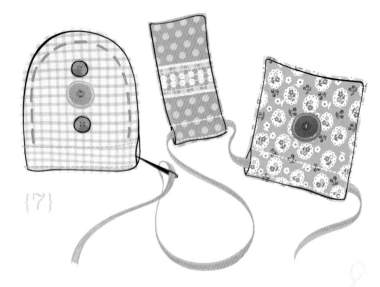

{7}

# Christmas stockings

If you've had your fill of stockings featuring Santa, Rudolph, and their friends, this lively duo offers a suitably festive alternative. The striped stocking ends in a laced sneaker, and the polka-dot one in a neatly buttoned Mary Jane. Both versions were made with contemporary quilting fabrics and lined with soft, cozy fleece. Some pom-pom trim around the top adds the finishing touch. Each stocking is about 18 inches (46 cm) tall, so they should be plenty big enough for all those little Christmas treats.

## You will need

*For each stocking*

✂ 22 x 25-inch (56 x 64-cm) piece of cotton fabric for the main stocking

✂ 22 x 25-inch (56 x 64-cm) piece of cream fleece fabric for the lining

✂ Sewing threads to match both fabrics

✂ 6-inch (15-cm) length of cotton tape, ½ inch (12 mm) wide

*For the sneaker stocking*

✂ 12-inch (31-cm) square of black felt

✂ Gray and black sewing threads

✂ 24-inch (61-cm) length of black shoelace

✂ 18-inch (46-cm) length of green pom-pom trim, ⅝ inch (1.5 cm) wide, and matching thread

✂ Light-colored quilter's pencil

*For the Mary Jane shoe stocking*

✂ 12-inch (31-cm) square of red felt

✂ Red sewing thread

✂ One ¾-inch (18-mm) white button

✂ 18-inch (46-cm) length of red pom-pom trim, ⅝ inch (1.5 cm) wide, and matching thread

✂ Templates on page 72

✂ Pencil

✂ Paper

✂ Basic sewing kit (see page 4)

# How to make the Christmas stocking

{1} Using the templates on page 72, cut out two outer pieces from your main fabric and two lining pieces from fleece for each stocking. For the sneaker stocking, cut out two pieces from black felt, using the sneaker template. For the Mary Jane stocking, cut out two pieces from red felt, using the Mary Jane template, plus a strip of red felt measuring ¾ x 7 inches (2 x 18 cm).

{2} Place one felt shoe piece on the right side of one main outer stocking piece and pin in place. Use your machine to sew around the top edge of the shoe shapes in straight stitch, close to the edge. For the sneaker, mark a curve for the toe piece with the quilter's pencil, 2 inches (5 cm) in from the edge. Work two lines in straight stitch on each side of the curve, using gray thread. Repeat to create the other side of the stocking.

{3} Place the two outer stocking pieces right sides together, making sure that the shoe parts line up. Pin in place, then machine stitch around the sides and bottom of the stocking in matching threads, changing the thread color, if necessary, and using a ⅜-inch (1-cm) seam allowance.

{4} Place the two fleece stocking pieces right sides together and machine stitch around the sides and bottom, using a ⅝-inch (1.5-cm) seam allowance and leaving a 4-inch (10-cm) gap along the lower edge; you will need this to turn the stocking right side out later on.

{5} Trim all the seam allowances to ¼ inch (6 mm).

{6} Turn the fleece lining right side out and insert it into the outer stocking, which should be wrong side out. Pin the lining and the outer stocking together around the top, making sure that the side seams match. Machine stitch around the top, using a ⅝-inch (1.5-cm) seam allowance.

{7} Turn the stocking right side out through the gap in the lining. Sewing by hand, slip-stitch the gap in the lining closed (see page 7).

{8} Press the outer stocking. Push the lining down into the outer stocking.

{9} Machine topstitch around the top edge of the stocking, ⅜ inch (1 cm) from the edge (see page 7).

{10} For the Mary Jane stocking, machine stitch around the strip of red felt for the strap. Stitch it in place at one side ⅜ inch (1 cm) down from the edge of the shoe. Secure the other side with the button. For the sneaker stocking, make three holes along each side of the sneaker, ⅝ inch (1.5 cm) down from the center seam, using the point of a small pair of scissors. Thread the shoelace through the holes, using the photograph on page 68 as a guide, and tie it in a bow.

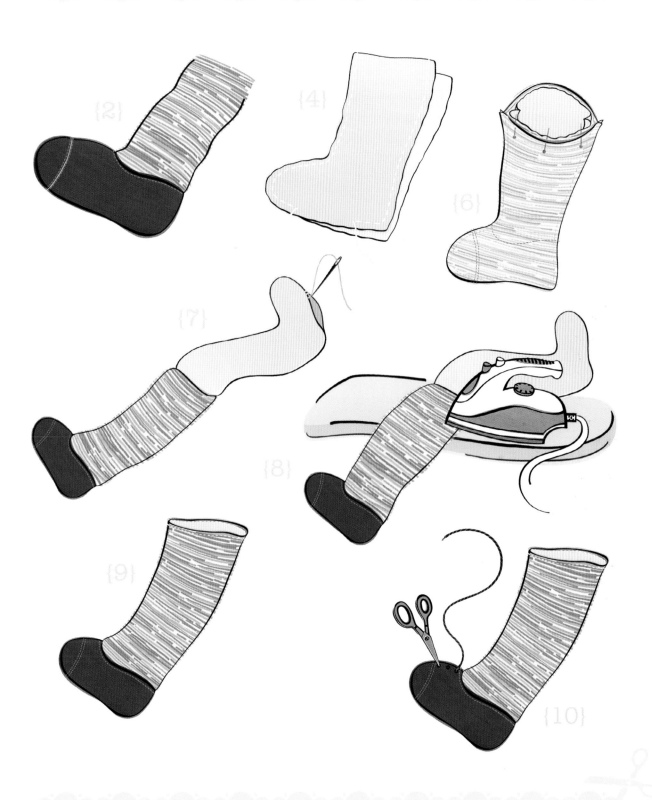

{2}

{4}

{6}

{7}

{8}

{9}

{10}

{11} Fold under ⅜ inch (1 cm) at one end of the length of cotton tape. Tuck the other end behind the folded end. Place the loop across the seam on the inside back of the stocking, just down from the top edge, so that the raw edge is concealed. Stitch it in place by working a small square of machine stitching.

{12} Pin the pom-pom trim around the top of the stocking, ⅜ inch (1 cm) down from the top, beginning and ending at the back seam and tucking the raw edges under at each end of the trim. Stitch in place through the outer part of the stocking only, using a hand running stitch and matching thread (see page 7).

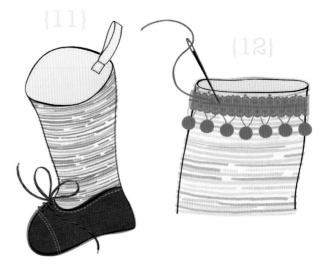

## Templates

Shown at 25%; enlarge by 400% for actual size.

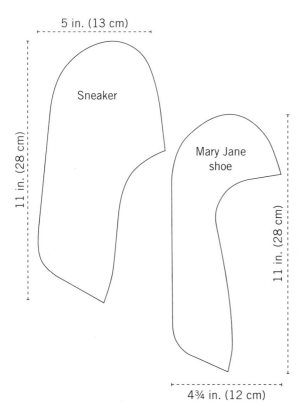

5 in. (13 cm)

Sneaker

11 in. (28 cm)

Mary Jane shoe

11 in. (28 cm)

4¾ in. (12 cm)

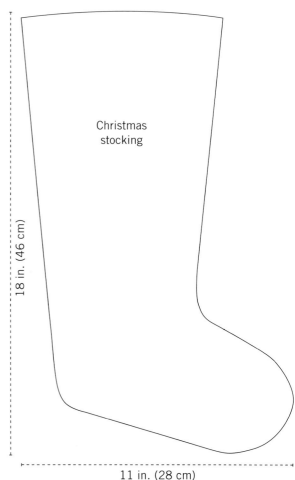

Christmas stocking

18 in. (46 cm)

11 in. (28 cm)

# Tree star

In most homes, the more densely decorated the Christmas tree the better. These tree stars can be hung or used as tree toppers—add a loop for hanging, or thread some cord through the back to tie the star to the top of your tree. They're simple enough to make a good family project to do with the kids. Choose a special selection of fabrics; they can be a great way to upcycle favorite prints on outgrown or worn-out clothes, which will give them instant nostalgia value. The star measures about 5 inches (13 cm) across.

## You will need

- ✂ Template on right
- ✂ Tracing paper and paper to make template
- ✂ Pencil
- ✂ One 8-inch (20-cm) square each of two contrasting cotton fabrics
- ✂ Cream thread and thread to match your fabrics
- ✂ Mother-of-pearl button, ⅝ inch (15 mm) in diameter
- ✂ 8-inch (20-cm) length of silver cord
- ✂ Small handful of polyester fabric filling
- ✂ Basic sewing kit (see page 4)

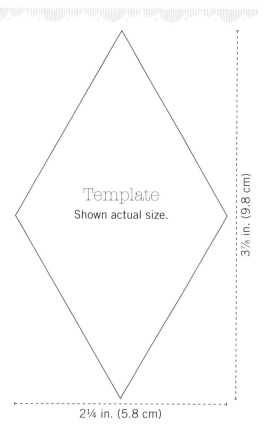

Template
Shown actual size.

3⅞ in. (9.8 cm)

2¼ in. (5.8 cm)

## How to make the tree star

[1] Using the template above, cut out six diamond shapes from each of your two fabrics. You will need three diamond shapes of each fabric to make each side of the star.

[2] Place two diamond shapes in contrasting fabrics right sides together. Using a ⅜-inch (1-cm) seam allowance, machine stitch the pieces together along one side. Press the seam open.

[3] Place the third diamond face down on the right side of a contrasting diamond. Machine stitch together, starting ⅜ inch (1 cm) from the top edge of the seam near the center.

[4] Repeat step 3 three times, so that the six diamonds are all sewn together.

[5] Fold the shape so that the first and last diamonds are right sides together. Machine stitch together, again using a ⅜-inch (1-cm) seam allowance.

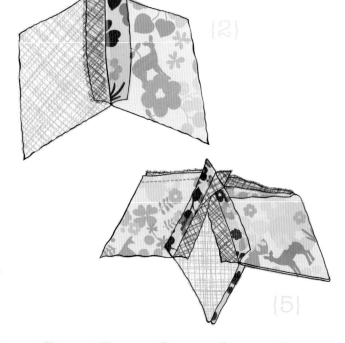

{2}

{5}

{6} Press all the seams open.

{7} Repeat steps 2–4 to make a second star shape. Then press under ⅜ inch (1 cm) along the two unsewn sides (the ones closest to the center) of the first and last diamonds. (This will form the gap for turning and stuffing once you have sewn the front and back star shapes together.)

{8} Pin the two star shapes right sides together. Machine stitch around the outer edge, using a ⅜-inch (1-cm) seam allowance. Clip the points (see page 7) and clip into the angles between the shapes, being careful not to snip into the stitching.

{9} Turn the star right side out through the gap and press.

{10} For a hanging star, thread the silver cord through the top of one of the star points from the inside, then thread it back down through the point in the same place. Knot the two ends together. If you are using your star as a tree topper instead of as a hanging decoration, thread the silver cord through the back of the star instead of the tip and use it to tie the star to the top of the tree.

{11} Stuff the star lightly. Sewing by hand, slip-stitch the gap closed (see page 7). Sew the button to the center front of the star, using cream thread and stitching through both sides of the star.

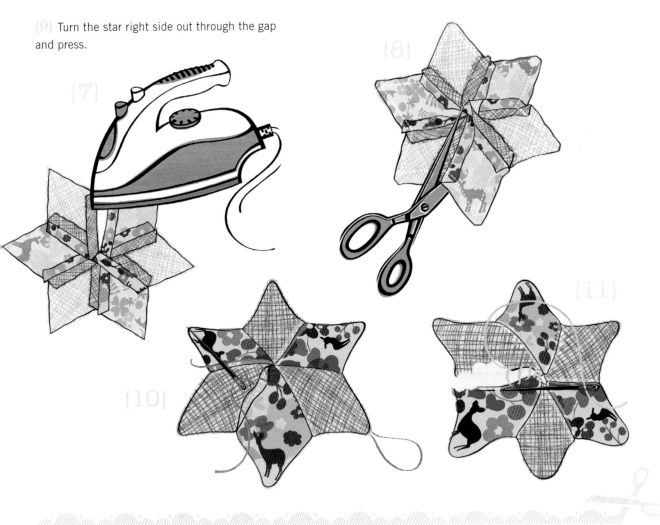

# Advent calendar

5–8 hrs

More sophisticated than your average chocolate Advent calendar, and with a lot more potential for interesting contents, this take on the traditional pre-Christmas treat is made from twenty-four little felt pockets strung out on a piece of ribbon. Our numbers have been made using quirky tape-measure print fabric and self-cover buttons, but you can vary this according to what you can find; try numbers cut from a real cloth tape measure or counters from an unloved game of bingo.

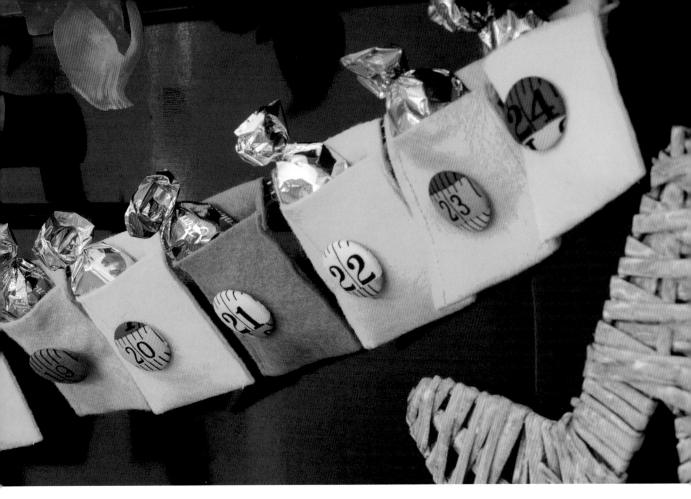

## You will need

✂ Template on page 78

✂ 24 pieces of felt, each measuring 2½ x 6 inches (6 x 15 cm); we used four rectangles of felt, each in a different shade and each measuring 8 x 12 inches (20 x 31 cm)

✂ Thread to match all your shades of felt

✂ 24 self-cover buttons, ⅞ inch (22 mm) in diameter

✂ Cotton fabric with tape-measure print; make sure your piece includes all the numbers you need

✂ 3¼-yard (3-m) length of narrow ribbon or tape

✂ Basic sewing kit (see page 4)

✂ Pair of pliers

✂ Tacky glue

✂ Medium-size safety pin

# How to make the Advent calender

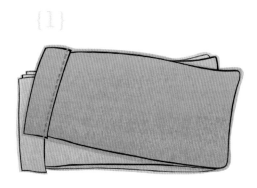

{1}

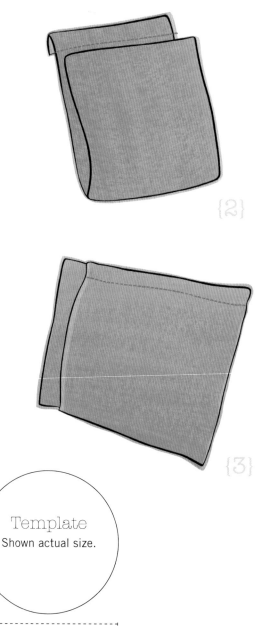

{2}

{3}

{1} Cut out all your felt rectangles. Fold down ¾ inch (2 cm) along one short edge of each piece, press in place, and then machine stitch close to the raw edge. This will form the casing for your ribbon or tape. The casing will be approximately ⅜ inch (1 cm) wide when finished.

{2} Turn the felt over so that the turned-down edge is on the underside. Turn up the other short edge to ⅜ inch (1 cm) below the folded edge of the casing.

{3} Machine stitch down each side of the pocket, close to the edges.

{4} Using the template below, cut out numbers 1 to 24 from the tape-measure fabric, making sure your numbers are centered on the circle.

## Template
Shown actual size.

|←----------------------------→|

1½ in. (3.8 cm)

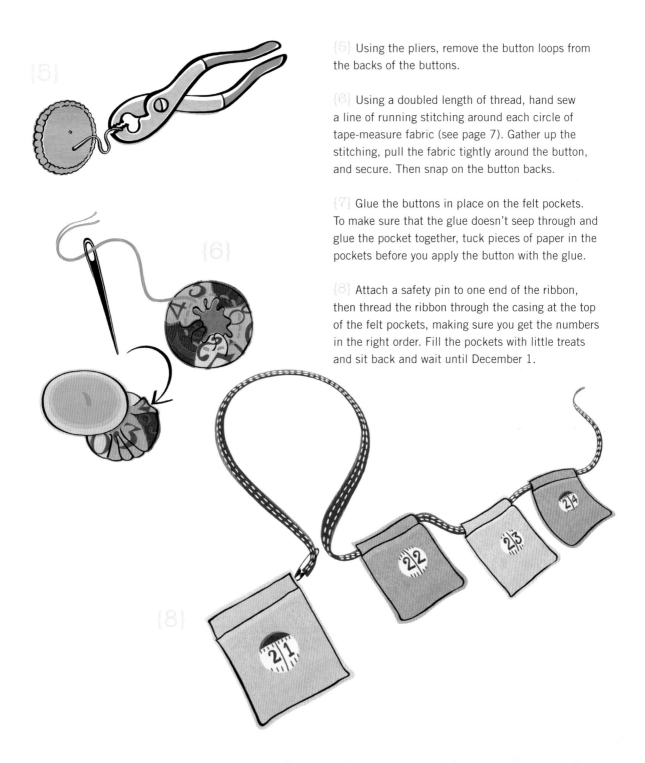

{5} Using the pliers, remove the button loops from the backs of the buttons.

{6} Using a doubled length of thread, hand sew a line of running stitching around each circle of tape-measure fabric (see page 7). Gather up the stitching, pull the fabric tightly around the button, and secure. Then snap on the button backs.

{7} Glue the buttons in place on the felt pockets. To make sure that the glue doesn't seep through and glue the pocket together, tuck pieces of paper in the pockets before you apply the button with the glue.

{8} Attach a safety pin to one end of the ribbon, then thread the ribbon through the casing at the top of the felt pockets, making sure you get the numbers in the right order. Fill the pockets with little treats and sit back and wait until December 1.

# Monster
# draft buster

5–8 hrs

When the wind starts whistling under the doors on a chilly evening, you know it's time to raid your fabric stash for some coordinated cottons to make this friendly monster draft buster. He's a change from the ubiquitous snake or sausage-dog designs and he's fast and straightforward to put together. Measure your door before you start and adjust the pattern up or down for a perfect draft blocker.

# You will need

- Templates on page 84
- Tracing paper and paper to make templates
- Pencil
- An assortment of coordinating cotton fabrics in the following amounts:
  Two 7 x 8¼-inch (18 x 21-cm) pieces for the head
  One 12 x 16½-inch (31 x 42-cm) piece for the middle body
  One 12 x 10½-inch (31 x 27-cm) piece for the end body
- Small pieces of the fabric you have chosen for the middle of the body for the ears and eye base, plus a small piece of the fabric you have chosen for the end of the body for the nose

- One 4¾ x 6-inch (12 x 15-cm) piece of natural linen for the face
- Small piece of cotton batting for the ears
- One 5 x 8¾-inch (13 x 22-cm) piece of fusible web
- Small black button and a medium-sized mother-of-pearl button for the eyes
- Sewing thread to match your fabrics
- Red sewing thread
- About 5½ ounces (150 g) polyester fiber filling
- Basic sewing kit (see page 4)
- Fabric marking pen

# How to make the monster draft buster

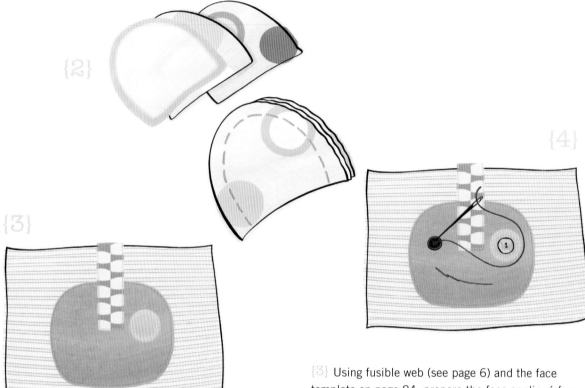

{1} Using the measurements on page 81, cut out two head pieces, one middle body piece, and one end body piece from your chosen fabrics. Using the templates on page 84, cut out four ear pieces from the same fabric as the middle body piece and two ear pieces from the batting.

{2} Place two ear pieces right sides together, with one of the batting ear pieces on top. Using a ⅜-inch (1-cm) seam allowance, machine stitch around the curved edge, leaving the straight edge open for turning. Trim the seam allowance, clip the curve (see page 7), turn the ear right side out, and press flat. Repeat for the second ear.

{3} Using fusible web (see page 6) and the face template on page 84, prepare the face appliqué from the natural linen. Cut out and apply it to the center of the front of one of the head pieces. Machine stitch around the face close to the edge, using matching thread. Make the nose appliqué from the same fabric as the end piece of the body. Press in place and machine stitch around the outer edge. Make the eye base appliqué from the same fabric as the middle body. Press in place and use the straight stitch on your sewing machine to sew a few lines around the outer edge.

{4} Using the fabric marking pen, draw the position of the mouth and left eye on the face. Using red thread and the straight stitch setting on your sewing machine, straight stitch over the mouth line four times. Sew on the buttons for the eyes.

{5}

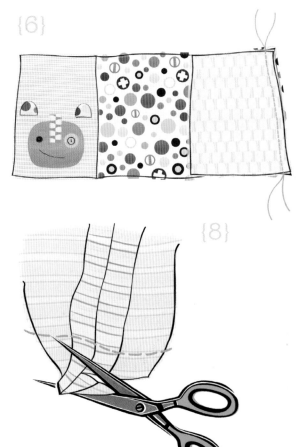

{6}

{8}

{5} Aligning the raw edges and with the ears pointing downward, pin the ears in place on the front head piece. Place the back and front head pieces right sides together and use your machine to sew across the top, using a ⅝-inch (1.5-cm) seam allowance. Press the seam open.

{6} With right sides together, pin and machine stitch the head piece to the middle body piece, using a ⅝-inch (1.5-cm) seam allowance. Pin and stitch the middle piece to the end body piece, again using a ⅝-inch (1.5-cm) seam allowance. Press the seams open.

{7} Fold the draft buster in half lengthwise, right sides together. Using a ⅝-inch (1.5-cm) seam allowance, use your machine to sew around the raw edges, leaving a 4-inch (10-cm) gap along the lower edge for turning and stuffing.

{8} To create a flat bottom for the lower edge of the face and the tail, flatten the lower left corner of the face into a point, so that the seams match at the center. Sew a straight line across the corner, 1 inch (2.5 cm) down from the pointed edge. Cut off the pointed edge. Repeat for the two corners at the end part of the draft buster.

{9} Turn the draft buster right side out, stuff, and slip-stitch the gap closed by hand (see page 7).

# Templates

Shown actual size.

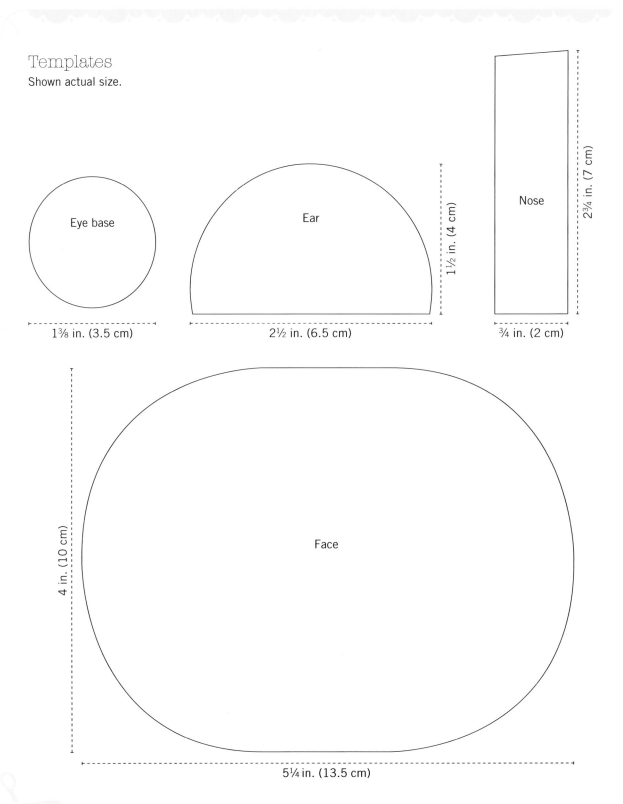

Eye base

1⅜ in. (3.5 cm)

Ear

2½ in. (6.5 cm)

1½ in. (4 cm)

Nose

¾ in. (2 cm)

2¾ in. (7 cm)

Face

4 in. (10 cm)

5¼ in. (13.5 cm)

# Bandana bib

Teddy bears and fluffy chicks are all too common on baby bibs. Tap into some cowboy chic instead, and whip up this version, cut from a genuine bandana, interlined with a piece of brushed cotton, and snapped securely in place at the back. The size given here should fit a baby up to about a year old. For bigger sizes, enlarge the pattern slightly—the bandana will still be large enough.

## You will need

✕ Template on page 87

✕ Pencil

✕ One standard-size cotton bandana, about 20 inches (51 cm) square

✕ One triangle of white brushed cotton, the same size as the bandana folded in half diagonally

✕ Sewing thread to match your fabric

✕ Black sewing thread

✕ One ⅝-inch (15-mm) snap fastener

✕ One ¾-inch (18-mm) white button

✕ Basic sewing kit (see page 4)

# How to make the baby bib

{1} Wash, dry, and press the bandana.

{2} Fold the bandana in half diagonally, so that the fold goes through the points of any square design of the bandana, press along the fold, then open the bandana out flat.

{3} Using the template for half a bandana piece on page 87, cut out two pieces of full bandana, one from each diagonal half, keeping the center point on the template in line with the diagonal fold.

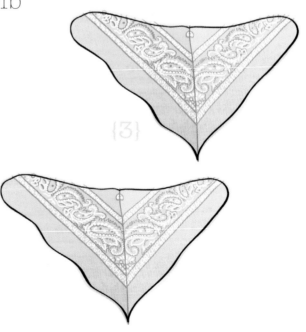

place on fold of fabric

11 in. (28 cm) diameter

Template
Shown at 50%; enlarge by 200% for actual size.

9 in. (22.5 cm) diameter

{4}

{8}

{4} Place the two bandana pieces right sides together. Lay them on top of the brushed cotton triangle. Pin through all three layers. Machine stitch around the outside edge of the bandana, using a ⅜-inch (1-cm) seam allowance and leaving a 4-inch (10-cm) gap along the center of one side for turning. Trim the brushed cotton to the edge of the bandana.

{5} Snip off the front tip of the bib, just to the outside of the seam (this will help to make the front tip of the finished bib neat and pointed). Turn the bib right side out through the gap and press. Sewing by hand, slip-stitch the gap closed (see page 7).

{6} Topstitch around the entire bib, ¼ inch (6 mm) from the edge (see page 7).

{7} Sew the bottom of the snap fastener in place on the right side of one back corner of the bib. Sew the top of the snap fastener in place on a corresponding part on the wrong side of the other back corner.

{8} Using black thread, sew the button in place on the top of the outside of the bandana, over the top part of the snap fastener.

# Takeout cup cozy

Everyone should have a personalized cozy: it will keep your coffee warm for longer, stop you from burning your hands on a too-hot drink, and also make sure that it doesn't get mixed up with anyone else's. The prototype is designed to fit a cup 4½ inches (11.5 cm) high, but it's easy to create a custom-made fit for the cups at your favorite coffee bar—just follow the simple instructions below.

## You will need

- ✂ Template on page 90 (or make your own—see right)
- ✂ Tracing paper and paper for template
- ✂ Pencil
- ✂ 4¾ x 11½-inch (12 x 29-cm) piece of pale pink felt
- ✂ 4¾ x 11½-inch (12 x 29-cm) piece of cotton fabric for the lining, plus a small piece of the same fabric for the mug motif
- ✂ 4¾ x 11½-inch (12 x 29-cm) piece of cotton batting for the interlining
- ✂ Two 4¾ x 11½-inch (12 x 29-cm) pieces of fusible web, plus a 2½-inch (6-cm) square of fusible web
- ✂ One ⅜ x 3¼-inch (1 x 8-cm) long strip of sew-on hook-and-loop tape
- ✂ Black sewing thread
- ✂ White sewing thread (if you are using white hook-and-loop tape)
- ✂ Sewing thread to match your fabrics
- ✂ Basic sewing kit (see page 4)
- ✂ Fabric marking pen

## Making your own template

To make a template for a cup of your chosen size, wash out an old takeout cup, cut a straight line down the side, remove the bottom, and spread the shape out. Following the curves of the piece, draw a line about ⅜ inch (1 cm) below the rim and ⅜ inch (1 cm) up from the lower edge. Trace this shape onto a piece of paper, then add ⅜ inch (1 cm) to each of the two straight sides.

## Template

Shown at 50%; enlarge by 200% for actual size.

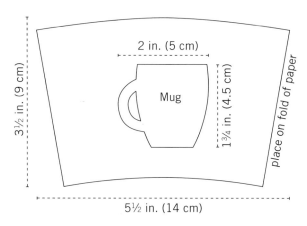

2 in. (5 cm)

Mug

3½ in. (9 cm)

1¾ in. (4.5 cm)

place on fold of paper

5½ in. (14 cm)

## How to work backstitch

Secure your thread by working a couple of stitches one over the other, then bring your needle out a stitch length along. Take your needle back down into your work at the end of your first stitch to create the back stitch. Then take it out another stitch length along past the previous stitch. Continue in this way until the line is complete.

# How to make the takeout cup cozy

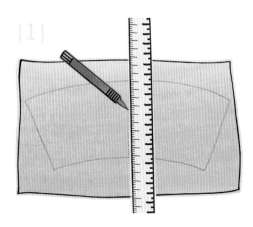

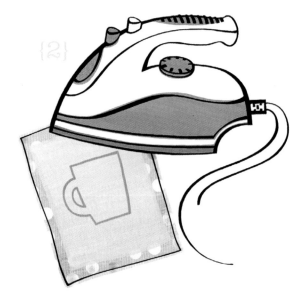

{1} Using the template above (or the one you have created), draw the cup cozy shape on the felt, but do not cut it out. Mark the center line as shown.

{2} Using the mug motif template above, the motif fabric, and the small square of fusible web, prepare the mug motif appliqué (see page 6).

{3} Cut out the appliqué motif and apply it to the center of the felt shape.

{4} Using black thread, sew around the mug motif close to the edge. We have used a sewing machine to do this, but if you do not feel confident sewing a small shape, you can sew it by hand instead, using running stitch (see page 7) or backstitch (see above).

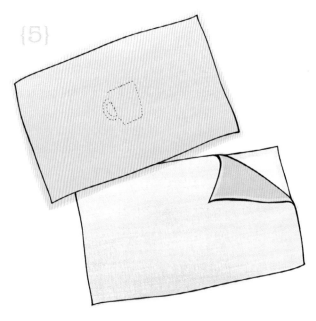

{5} Press the fusible web, glue side down, onto one side of the batting. Peel the backing paper off the fusible web, then press the batting down onto the reverse of the felt (the side without the mug motif).

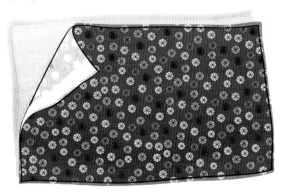

{6} Press the second rectangle of fusible web, glue side down, onto the reverse of the rectangle of lining fabric. Peel the backing paper off the fusible web and press the lining fabric down onto the batting.

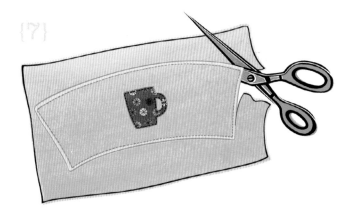

{7} Using matching thread, machine stitch around the entire cup cozy shape, just inside the template border. Cut along the template border. Spray or dab with water to remove the fabric marking pen marks.

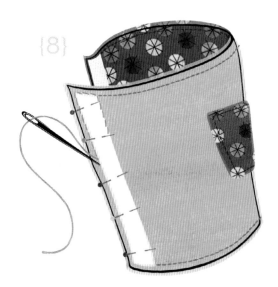

{8} Overcast the hook side of the hook-and-loop tape onto the left-hand edge of the front of the cozy by hand (see page 7). Overcast the loop side of the hook-and-loop tape onto the right-hand edge of the reverse of the cozy.

# Bird coasters

Bring a dash of contemporary style to your coffee table with a flock of silhouette bird coasters. We liked the slightly mismatched look of different colors of felt—but they'd work just as well made all in the same shade. There's a thick layer of batting sandwiched into the middle of the coasters to make them more substantial and to be sure that they are heat resistant. The coasters are speedy to make—particularly after you've mastered your first one—and they're an ideal way of using up tiny scraps of favorite fabrics. Each coaster measures just larger than 4 inches (10 cm) in diameter.

## You will need

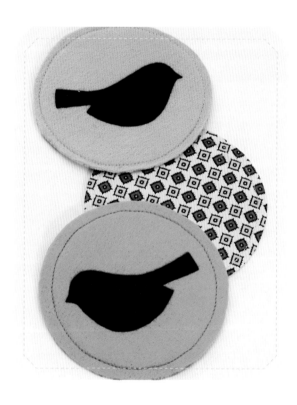

*For each coaster*

- ✂ Templates on page 94
- ✂ Tracing paper and paper for template
- ✂ Pencil
- ✂ One 4½-inch (11-cm) square of colored felt
- ✂ One 2¼ x 3½-inch (5.5 x 9-cm) piece of charcoal gray felt
- ✂ One 4½-inch (11-cm) square of cotton fabric to coordinate with your felt
- ✂ One 3¾-inch (9.5-cm) square of cotton batting
- ✂ Two 4½-inch (11-cm) squares and one 2¼ x 3½-inch (5.5 x 9-cm) piece of fusible web
- ✂ Charcoal gray or black thread
- ✂ Thread to match the colored felt
- ✂ Basic sewing kit (see page 4)
- ✂ Fabric marking pen

# How to make the bird coasters

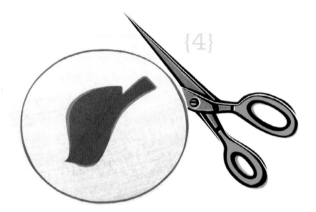

[1] Using the fabric marking pen and template A below, draw around the shape on your colored felt but do not cut it out.

[2] Using the small rectangle of fusible web and charcoal felt, prepare the bird appliqué on the charcoal gray felt (see page 6). Cut out the motif and apply it to the coaster in the position shown on the template.

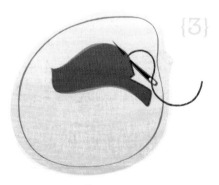

[3] Using charcoal or black thread and a small running stitch (see page 7), stitch around the bird shape by hand.

[4] Place one of the squares of fusible web, glue side down, on the reverse side of the square of felt with the bird appliqué. Iron in position (see page 6). Cut out the coaster shape.

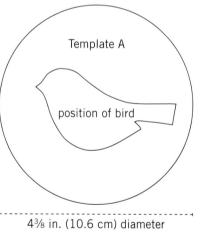

Template A

position of bird

4⅜ in. (10.6 cm) diameter

## Templates
Shown at 50%; enlarge by 200% for actual size.

Template B

3½ in. (9 cm) diameter

{5} Using the fabric marking pen and template B on the opposite page, draw around the shape on the piece of batting and cut out.

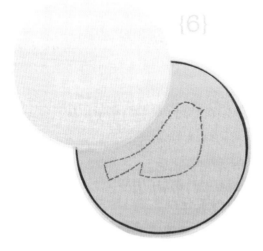

{6} Peel the backing paper off the fusible web that is attached to the reverse of the coaster and place the circle of batting in the center.

## Tip

As a precaution, you can place the paper from the fusible-web square over the coaster before you iron, so that the glue from the fusible web doesn't get on your iron.

{7} Iron the second square of fusible web onto the reverse side of the cotton fabric square. Peel the backing paper off the fusible web and lay the front part of the coaster, together with the batting, right side up on top. Iron the front of the coaster in place, being careful that the glue from the fusible web on the fabric square does not get onto the iron.

{8} Trim away the excess fabric so that the cotton on the reverse of the coaster matches the felt shape on the front. Using either a machine or sewing running stitches by hand, and using matching thread, sew around the coaster.

# Table runner

5-8 hrs

If you're looking for something classic and beautiful to adorn your table, this Scandinavian-inspired linen runner will meet the need. It's a sophisticated design that's still simple enough to run up in an afternoon. For the leaves, choose a fabric that coordinates with your tableware—small prints work best. Our runner is 6 feet (1.8 m) long, but you can adjust the pattern, adding or subtracting pairs of leaves, to make it a customized fit for your own dining table.

## You will need

- ✂ 81 x 19-inch (206 x 48-cm) piece of linen fabric
- ✂ Generous one-quarter (18 x 22 inches/46 x 56 cm) patterned quilting cotton
- ✂ 18 x 22-inch (46 x 56-cm) piece of fusible web
- ✂ 5½-yard (5-m) length of white rickrack trim, ⅜ inch (1 cm) wide
- ✂ Seven assorted small to medium white buttons
- ✂ Sewing thread to match the linen fabric and rickrack trim
- ✂ Green sewing thread
- ✂ Fabric marking pen
- ✂ Template on page 98
- ✂ Pencil
- ✂ Paper
- ✂ Ruler
- ✂ Basic sewing kit (see page 4)

# How to make the table runner

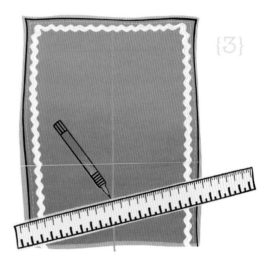

{1} Fold under ⅝ inch (1.5 cm) along each long edge of the linen fabric and press. Fold under another ⅝ inch (1.5 cm) and press again. Do the same along the short edges. Tuck in the corners of the short edges and press again. Machine stitch all around the edge of the fabric, close to the inside folded edge, using matching thread.

{2} Sew rickrack trim around the entire runner, just in from the inside edge. Your stitching should be across the center of the rickrack trim and it is easiest to start sewing in the middle of one side instead of at a corner. At the corners, sew to a point just before the end, then, with the needle still in the fabric, raise the machine foot and bring the trim up and over at a right angle, then lower the machine foot again and continue sewing.

## Template

Shown at 50%; enlarge by 200% for actual size.

{3} Using a fabric marking pen, mark a line down the center of the runner. Measure 1¼ inches (3 cm) from one end of the center line and make a mark. This will be the start of the stem. Measure 5 inches (13 cm) from the first mark to make a second mark. This will be where the first pair of leaves will be attached to the stem. Measure 9 inches (23 cm) from this mark and make another mark for the placement of the second pair of leaves. Do this another five times, spacing the marks 9 inches (23 cm) apart, to mark where five more pairs of leaves will be placed. Measure 6¼ inches (16 cm) from the last mark to make the final mark for the position of the bottom of a single leaf.

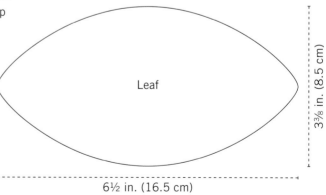

Leaf

3⅜ in. (8.5 cm)

6½ in. (16.5 cm)

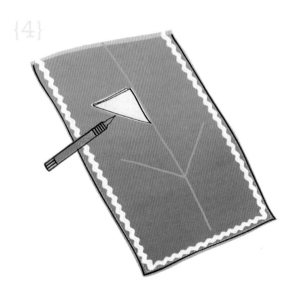

{4} Fold the short edge of a standard-size sheet of paper to one of its long edges to make a 45-degree angle. By placing the paper along the center line and drawing along the angle, make pairs of 6¼-inch (16 cm) lines at 45-degree angles up and away from the stem at each of the seven marks you made for the pairs of leaves.

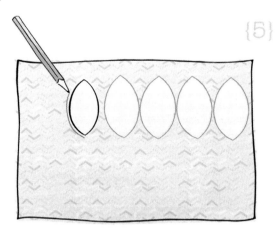

{5} Create your copy of the template on page 98. Press the fusible web onto the wrong side of the quilting fabric and draw around the template to make 15 leaf appliqués (see page 6).

{6} Following the instructions on page 6, iron the leaves along the center line so that the tops and bottoms of the leaves are on the 45-degree lines and there is a slight gap between the bottoms of the leaves. The bottom of the top leaf should be on the top mark. Using green thread and starting at the bottom of the stem, machine straight stitch up to the first pair of leaves. Stitch around the pair of leaves. Repeat the stitching up the stem and around each pair of leaves until you reach the final leaf. Stitch around the top leaf, then stitch up and down the stem a couple of times more before finishing.

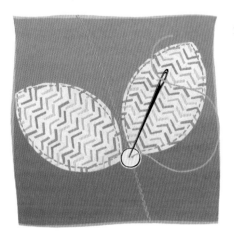

{7} Stitch a button in place at the bottom of each pair of leaves and at the bottom of the top leaf.

# Apron

One-size-fits-all aprons tend, exasperatingly, not to fit anyone well—but this model is an exception. Now everyone can cut a sartorial dash in the kitchen. The head loop and waist ties are a continuous length of tape, threaded through channels on the sides of the apron bib, so you can adjust the whole thing to fit anyone from a biggish child to a large adult. Add an appliqué of your choice and you have a completely personalized product that you'll enjoy wearing. If you feel like it, you could even make a set—one for each member of the family—to encourage cooperative cooking efforts.

## You will need

✂ Templates on page 105

✂ Tracing paper and paper for templates

✂ Pencil

✂ 35½-inch (90-cm) piece of printed linen fabric at least 45 inches (115 cm) wide

✂ 3¼-yard (3-m) length of linen tape, 1 inch (2.5 cm) wide

✂ 5 x 9-inch (13 x 23-cm) piece of cotton fabric for the appliqué

✂ 5 x 9-inch (13 x 23-cm) piece of fusible web

✂ Thread to match your fabric

✂ White button, ¾ inch (20 mm) in diameter

✂ Basic sewing kit (see page 4)

✂ Fabric marking pen

✂ Large safety pin for threading the ties

# How to make the apron

{1} Using the guide on page 6, cut out the templates (see page 105). Use the templates to cut out your apron fabric: you will need one main piece and two facings. Remember to cut out one facing using your template the right way up and one using your template face down.

{2} Lay the main apron piece right side up on your work surface, with one of the facings right side down on top, aligning the raw edges. Pin together and machine stitch, using a ⅜-inch (1-cm) seam allowance. Sew the other facing on in the same way. Clip into the curves (see page 7) and press the seams open.

{3} If your fabric is prone to fraying, zigzag stitch along the raw edges of the facings. Then fold under ⅜ inch (1 cm) along these edges. Press in place.

{4} Fold under ⅜ inch (1 cm) along the top edge of the apron, including the facings, and press. Fold under another ⅜ inch (1 cm) and press again. Machine stitch close to the lower folded edge.

{5} Fold under ⅜ inch (1 cm) along both sides of the apron, including the facings, and press. Fold under another ⅜ inch (1 cm) and press again. Machine stitch close to the inner folded edge.

{6} Fold the facings in and press. Pin in place, then machine stitch close to the inside folded edge along the long edges of the facings to form casings for the apron straps.

{7} Fold up ⅜ inch (1 cm) along the lower edge and press. Fold up ⅝ inch (1.5 cm) and press again. Machine stitch close to the upper folded edge.

{8} Cut out a piece of 11 x 16-inch (28 x 41 cm) fabric for the pocket. Turn under ⅜ inch (1 cm) along the lower edge and press. Turn under another ⅜ inch (1 cm) and press again. Machine stitch close to the top of the folded edge. Repeat along the two sides.

{9} Turn under ⅜ inch (1 cm) along the top edge of the pocket and press. Turn under another 1½ inches (4 cm) and press again. Machine stitch close to the lower folded edge.

{10} Using the printed cotton and fusible web, prepare the fish appliqué motif (see page 6). Cut out the motif and apply it to the pocket, centered on the pocket width and with the lower edge of the fish about 2½ inches (6 cm) up from the lower edge of the pocket.

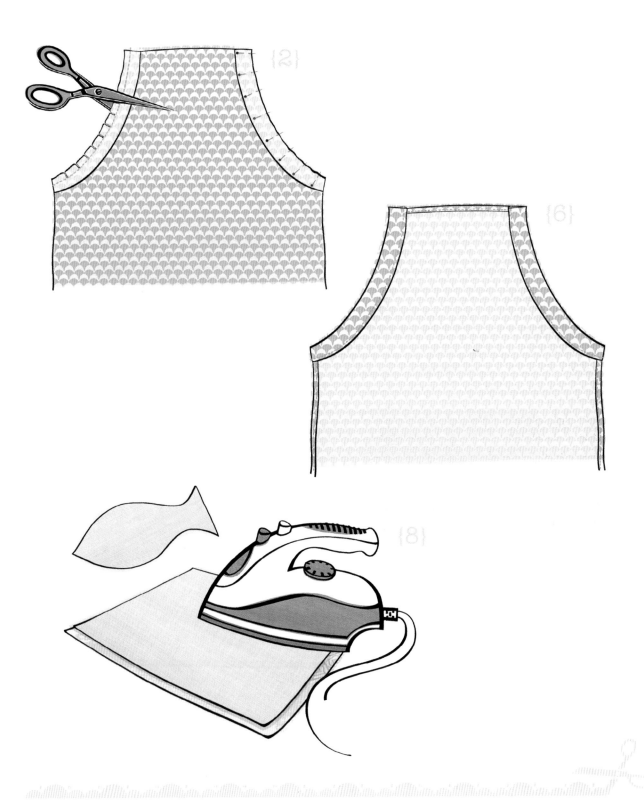

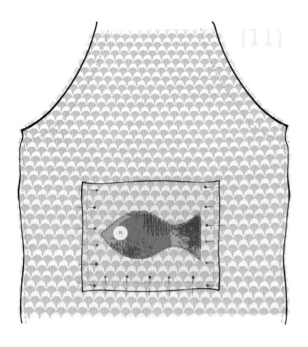

{11} Pin the pocket in the center of the apron, 6 inches (15 cm) up from the bottom. Machine stitch around the sides and lower edge of the pocket, close to the edge, reverse stitching at the top edges to make sure it is secure (see page 7).

{12} Sew on the button for the fish's eye.

{13} Attach a safety pin to one end of the linen tape. Thread the tape up through the lower edge of one of the side casings and out through the top, then thread the tape back down through the top of the second side casing and out through the lower edge.

{14} Fold under 1 inch (2.5 cm) at each end of the tape and press. Fold under another 1 inch (2.5 cm) and press again. Sew around the tape in a square shape. Adjust the tape to fit.

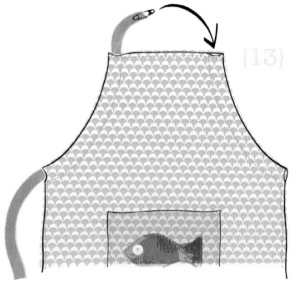

## Templates

Shown at 20%; enlarge by
500% for actual size.

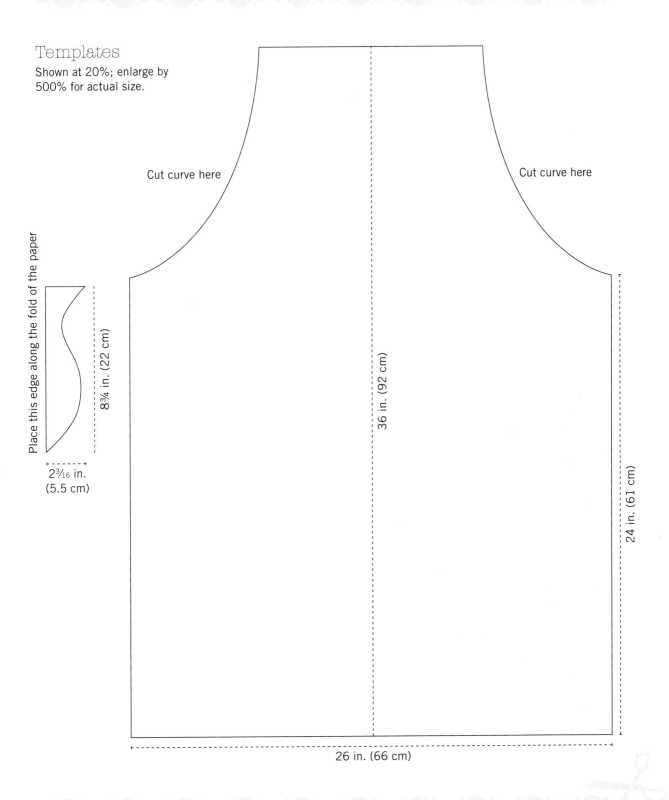

Place this edge along the fold of the paper

8¾ in. (22 cm)

2³⁄₁₆ in.
(5.5 cm)

Cut curve here

Cut curve here

36 in. (92 cm)

24 in. (61 cm)

26 in. (66 cm)

# Sarong

Is it a skirt? Is it a dress? Is it a beach wrap? It's all three, of course, because it's a sarong. Made from a simple piece of hemmed fabric, it's hardly surprising that the sarong is one of the most popular items of clothing worldwide. We added a border to ours because we thought it would be a great way to make a small-but-beautiful remnant of a floral-patterned cotton fabric work a lot harder, and we made a neat travel bag to put it in, too. For the simplest version possible, however, you could just hem the right size piece of fabric and be ready to go.

## You will need

*For the sarong*

- ✂ 38 x 56-inch (97 x 142-cm) piece of cream cotton or cotton mixture fabric
- ✂ 28 x 56-inch (71 x 142-cm) piece of floral-patterned cotton fabric
- ✂ Stranded pink embroidery thread to coordinate with the floral-patterned cotton fabric
- ✂ Cream sewing thread

*For the travel bag*

- ✂ Template on page 110
- ✂ Tracing paper and paper for template
- ✂ Pencil
- ✂ Two 8 x 12-inch (20 x 31-cm) pieces of cream cotton or cotton mixture fabric
- ✂ Leftovers crap of floral-printed cotton from making the sarong
- ✂ Small piece of fusible web
- ✂ 4-foot (120 cm) length of pale blue ribbon, ¼ inch (6 mm) wide

- ✂ Cream sewing thread
- ✂ Basic sewing kit (see page 4)
- ✂ Fabric marking pen
- ✂ Small safety pin for threading the ribbon of the travel bag

# How to make the sarong

{1} Cut your floral-patterned cotton lengthwise into four equal strips. With right sides together, aligning the raw edges, pin one patterned cotton strip to one long side of the main piece. Machine stitch together, using a ⅜-inch (1-cm) seam allowance. Repeat for the other long side. Press the seams toward the patterned cotton strips.

{2}

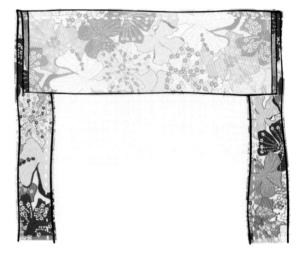

{3} Fold under ⅝ inch (1.5 cm) on one short edge of the third border piece and press. With right sides together, aligning the long raw edges, pin the border piece to a short side of the main piece. Trim the border piece so that it extends ⅝ inch (1.5 cm) beyond the edge of the main piece. Fold the extending edge under to align with the main piece and press.

{4} Machine stitch the border in place, using a ⅜-inch (1-cm) seam allowance, and press the seam toward the patterned cotton fabric. Repeat steps 3 and 4 to make the border for the second short side.

{2} Fold under ⅜ inch (1 cm) along the raw edge of one of the border pieces and press. Fold the border over so that the folded edge overlaps the seam by just under 1/16 inch (2 mm). Pin on the right side, then machine stitch down this line. Repeat for the other border.

{5}

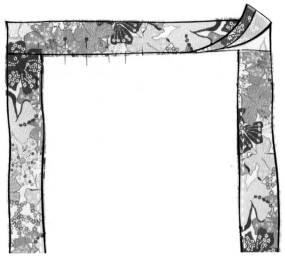

{5} Fold under ⅜ inch (1 cm) along the raw edge of one of the short borders and press. Fold the border over so that the folded edge overlaps the seam by just under ¹⁄₁₆ inch (2 mm). Pin on the right side, then machine stitch down this line. Repeat for the other border.

{6} Slip-stitch the gaps at the corners closed by hand (see page 7).

## Wear it in all kinds of ways

For loads of ideas on the different ways you can wear your sarong, just type "how to wear a sarong" into your favorite search engine. After checking out the results, you certainly won't be short of ideas.

{7}

{7} Using the fabric marking pen, draw a line all around the main cream part of the sarong, just over ¼ inch (6 mm) from the seam line between the main fabric and the border pieces. Sewing by hand and using three strands of pink embroidery thread, work over this line in a medium-length running stitch (see page 7).

# Travel bag

{1} Using your sewing machine, zigzag stitch around all four sides of the two cream rectangles.

{2} Using the template below, the fusible web, and the scrap of border fabric, prepare the heart appliqué motif (see page 6). Cut out the appliqué motif and apply it to the center of one of the pieces of cream fabric, 2¾ inches (7 cm) up from one of the short edges. Straight stitch around the edge of the appliqué, using cream thread.

{3} Place the two cream rectangles right sides together. Using the fabric marking pen, make marks ¾ inch (2 cm) and 1¾ inches (4.5 cm) down from the top edge on both sides of the rectangles. Machine stitch around the sides and bottom of the bag, using a ⅜-inch (1-cm) seam allowance and leaving gaps between the two marks on each side. Press the side seams open.

{4} Turn down ⅜ inch (1 cm) all the way around the top edge and press. Then fold down again so that the top mark aligns with the bottom mark and press. Machine stitch around the top edge close to the lower folded edge. Turn the bag right side out and press.

{5} Divide the ribbon into two equal lengths. Attach a small safety pin to one end of one length, then feed the ribbon through the channel all the way around from the hole in one of the side seams and knot the ends together. Thread the other piece of ribbon all the way around from the other side and, again, knot the ends together.

## Template

Shown at 50%; enlarge by 200% for actual size.

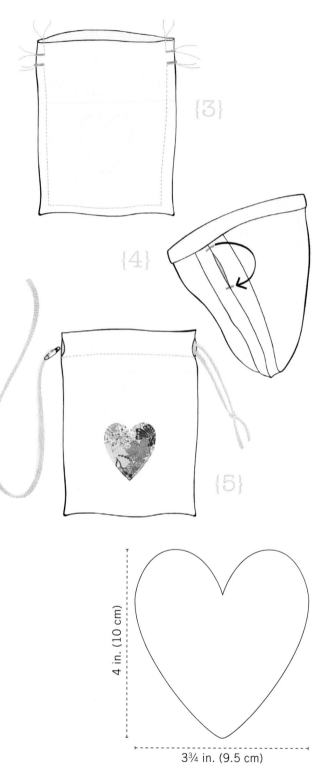

4 in. (10 cm)

3¾ in. (9.5 cm)

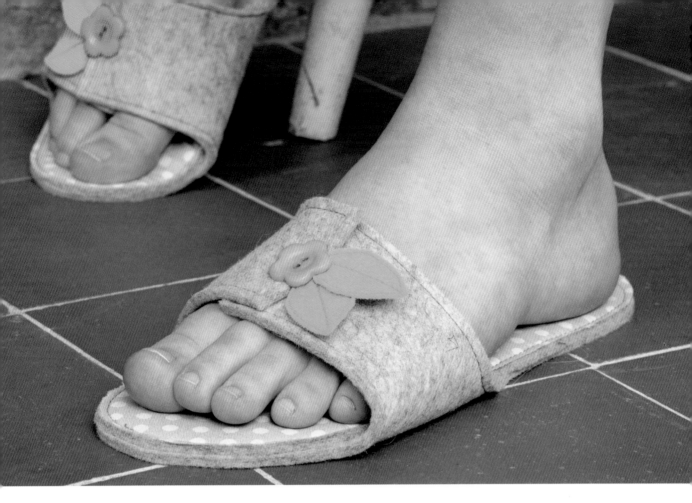

# Felt sandals

5–8 hrs

Creating your own footwear can be easier than it sounds—and this way
of making a good warm pair of indoor sandals is speedy indeed. You use an
existing pair of sandals or flip-flops as a pattern, so a great fit is a given, and
they're crafted from thick felt (easily available online). The basic shoe is created
from a single piece; you cut the straps as part of the main shoe and stitch them
together at the top. And you can make them in any size, from small kid to large
adult, and embellish (or not) to suit. Read on to see just how simple it is.

## You will need

- ✂ Pair of simple thong sandals or similar to use as a template
- ✂ Template on page 113
- ✂ Tracing paper and paper for template
- ✂ Pencil
- ✂ Two 12-inch (31-cm) squares of fusible web
- ✂ One 12-inch (31-cm) square of gray polka-dot cotton fabric
- ✂ 17 x 23-inch (43 x 58-cm) piece of pale gray felt, about 1/8 inch (4 mm) thick
- ✂ Small piece of standard-size green felt
- ✂ Two flower-shape pink buttons
- ✂ Gray and green sewing threads
- ✂ Basic sewing kit (see page 4)
- ✂ Fabric marking pen

## How to make the felt sandals

[1] Using your existing sandals as a template, draw around the right and left sandals on one of the pieces of fusible web. Place the fusible web, glue side down, on the reverse of the gray polka-dot cotton fabric, iron in place, and cut out the sandal linings.

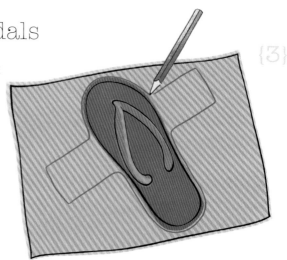

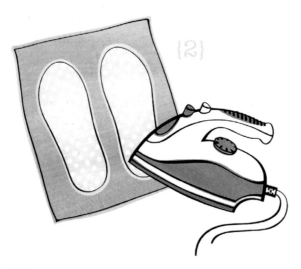

[2] Peel off the backing paper from the linings and place them glue side down on the gray felt. Press in place. Cut your felt to match the linings to create the sandal insoles.

[3] You will need to make a template for the bottom and the straps of each sandal. Put one of your sandals on a piece of brown paper and draw around it. Add a 2 x 3½-inch (5 x 9-cm) rectangle on each side for the straps in the place where you want the strap to come across your foot. Use these templates to cut two outer sandal pieces from the pale gray felt.

{4} Machine stitch around the strap part of the outer sandal pieces in gray thread, ¼ inch (6 mm) from the edges, making sure that your stitching begins and ends in the center of the curves.

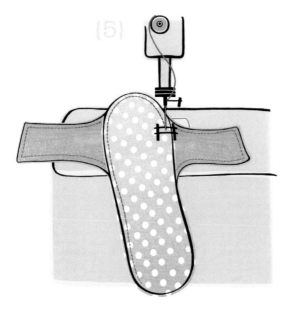

{5} Place the insole pieces right side up on the top of your main sandal shapes and pin in place. Machine stitch around the insole in gray thread, ¼ inch (6 mm) from the edge.

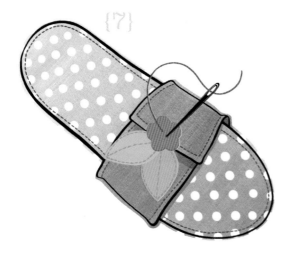

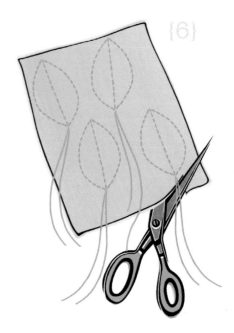

{6} Use the leaf template below and the fabric marking pen to create the outlines of four leaves on the green felt. Machine stitch around the edges of the shapes in green thread, beginning and ending your stitching at one end of the leaves. Sew two lines down the center of each leaf, ending your stitching at the same end of the leaves. Cut around the leaves carefully, leaving your thread tails intact.

{7} Overlap the straps of the sandals so that the inside strap is uppermost and pin in place. Stitch the leaves and the button in place, catching the two straps of the sandal together as you do so to secure them.

## Template
Shown actual size.

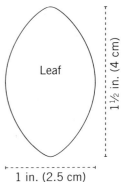

Leaf

1½ in. (4 cm)

1 in. (2.5 cm)

# Baby shoes

These are the easiest baby shoes you could ever make. There are just
two pattern pieces and no complicated elastic or fastenings. The fleece lining
helps them to stay put on little feet as well as keeping your baby cozy on cool
days. The shoe template is supplied in two sizes, so you can make the shoes
for babies up to three months or from three to six months.

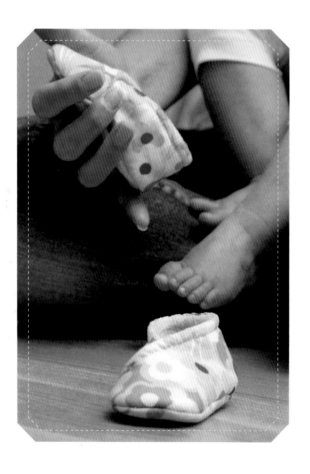

## You will need

✂ Templates on page 116

✂ Pencil

✂ Paper

✂ 12 x 18-inch (31 x 46-cm) piece of patterned
cotton fabric

✂ 12 x 18-inch (31 x 46-cm) piece fleece in a color
that is coordinated with the cotton fabric

✂ Matching sewing thread

✂ Basic sewing kit (see page 4)

# How to make the baby shoes

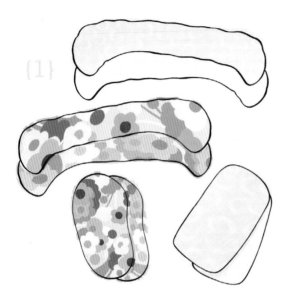

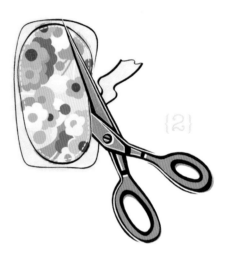

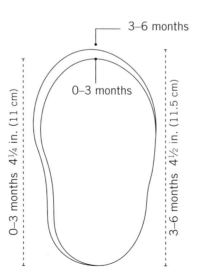

{1} Pin your copies of the templates below to the fabric and cut out two top pieces and two sole pieces from your patterned cotton fabric, remembering to cut one sole piece with the template face up and the other with it face down. Cut out two top pieces and two rectangles that are slightly bigger than the sole pieces from the fleece.

{2} With wrong sides together, pin the outer fabric sole pieces to the fleece rectangles. Machine stitch around the outer sole pieces, very close to the edge. Trim the fleece rectangles to the same size as the outer fabric soles.

## Template
Shown at 50%; enlarge by 200% for actual size.

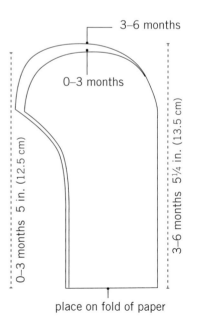

3–6 months

0–3 months

0–3 months 4¼ in. (11 cm)

3–6 months 4½ in. (11.5 cm)

3–6 months

0–3 months

0–3 months 5 in. (12.5 cm)

3–6 months 5¼ in. (13.5 cm)

place on fold of paper

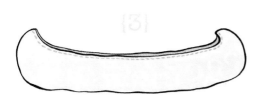

{3} Place one outer and one fleece top piece right sides together. Machine stitch along the top edge, using a ¼-inch (6-mm) seam allowance. Turn right side out and press lightly on the outer fabric. Topstitch along the top edge just over ¼ inch (6 mm) from the edge.

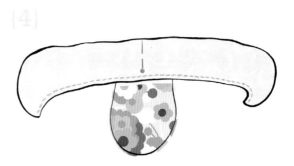

{4} Place the sole and top piece right sides together and pin the center of the top piece to the center of the back of the heel.

{5} Starting from the center of the heel, pin one side of the top piece around the outer side of the shoe, across the front, and then down the first part of the inner side. Machine stitch in place, using a ¼-inch (6-mm) seam allowance.

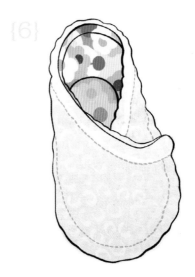

{6} Pin the other side of the top piece in position and stitch in place, again using a ¼-inch (6-mm) seam allowance. Work a zigzag stitch around the seam allowance.

{7} Turn the shoe right side out. Repeat steps 3–7 to make the second shoe, remembering that it will be a mirror image of the shoe you have just made.

# Lavender underwear sachet

A cute update on the classic lavender bag, to keep your clothes drawers sweet smelling (and moth free). You can't have too many (and they make good stocking stuffers, too), so mix up different prints and trims and use the patterns to appliqué them with panties and underpants in a range of styles and various colors and textures. Lavender sachets last much longer when they're lavishly filled, so try to lay your hands on a generous supply of lavender flowers. The sachets measure about 2 x 3¼ inches (5 x 8 cm).

## You will need

*For each lavender sachet*

✂ Templates on page 121

✂ Tracing paper and paper for template

✂ Pencil

✂ Two rectangles of natural linen, each measuring 4½ x 6 inches (11.5 x 15 cm)

✂ 2¾ x 4-inch (7 x 10-cm) piece of printed cotton

✂ 2¾ x 4-inch (7 x 10-cm) piece of fusible web

✂ Thread to match your natural linen

✂ Thread to contrast with your printed cotton

✂ Small store-bought white bow and a mother-of-pearl button ¼ inch (6 mm) in diameter (only for the girl's panties)

✂ Tiny white button (only for the boy's boxer shorts)

✂ 3 tablespoons of dried lavender flowers

✂ Basic sewing kit (see page 4)

✂ Teaspoon

# How to make the lavender underwear sachets

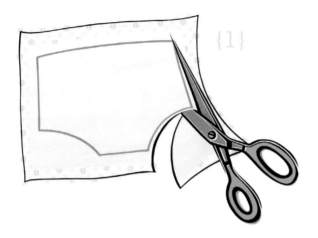

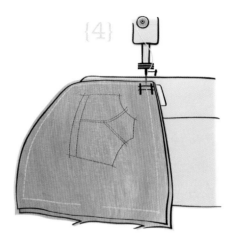

{1} Using your chosen template on page 121, the printed cotton, and the fusible web, prepare your chosen underwear appliqué motif (see page 6) and cut it out.

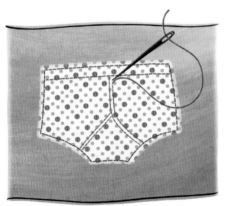

{2} Peel off the backing paper and press the appliqué onto the center of the right side of one of the linen rectangles. Machine stitch around the appliqué in contrasting thread, using the template and photos on pages 118–119 as a guide.

{3} Referring to the photos on pages 118–119, decorate the front of the sachet with a tiny ribbon bow or button.

{4} Place the two rectangles of linen right sides together and machine stitch around the outside, using a ⅜-inch (1-cm) seam allowance and leaving a 2-inch (5-cm) gap in one side for turning and filling.

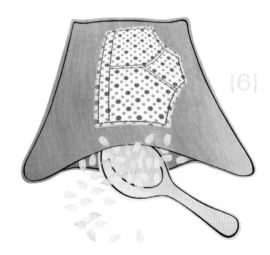

{5} Clip the corners of the sachet (see page 7), turn it right side out through the gap in the side, and press.

{6} Using a teaspoon, fill the sachet with lavender flowers. Slip-stitch the gap closed by hand (see page 7).

# Templates
Shown actual size.

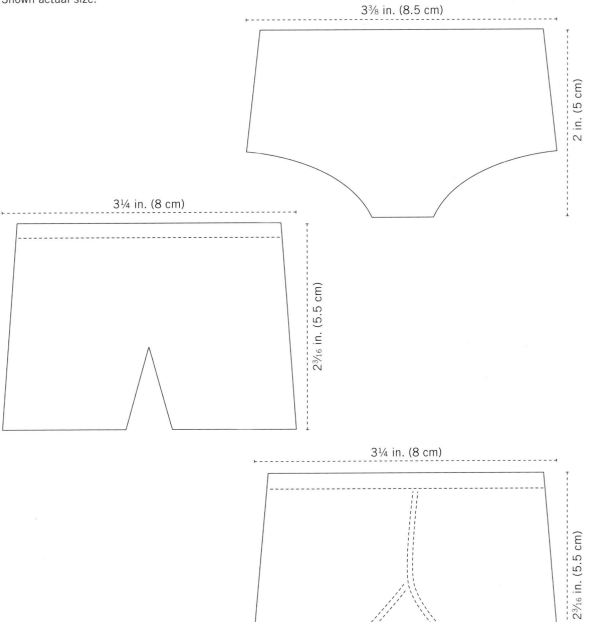

3⅜ in. (8.5 cm)

2 in. (5 cm)

3¼ in. (8 cm)

2³⁄₁₆ in. (5.5 cm)

3¼ in. (8 cm)

2³⁄₁₆ in. (5.5 cm)

# Wrap skirt

Most people who sew have, at one time or another, seen some great
fabric, thought about sewing a skirt ... and then changed their mind. It's the fatal
combination of darts, a tricky zipper, and a complicated waistband that does it. So
here is a pattern for a skirt that doesn't require any of those things, cut on the bias
for extra swing, and flattering to a wide range of shapes and sizes. It's comfortable
to wear, too, so once you've made one, you'll want to make several. Vary them with
different prints, textures, and trimmings.

## Sizing

The skirt will fit women in sizes 6–12,
depending on where you sew the second tie
(this will become clear a little later). It is
21½ inches (55 cm) long, which means it will
be about knee length on an average-height
woman when worn 2 inches (5 cm) or so below
the natural waistline. If you want a larger or
smaller size, just make the pieces a little wider
or narrower—this isn't couture tailoring. You
could also easily make it a little shorter or
longer by extending the shape at the bottom.
However, remember that if you make it longer,
you will need more fabric and extra trimming.

## You will need

✂ Templates on page 127

✂ Tracing paper and paper for templates

✂ Pencil

✂ 60-inch (1.5-m) piece of fabric that is at least
44 inches (111 cm) wide; you will need more
if the pattern on your fabric has a repeat of more
than a few inches

✂ 2½-yard (2.2-m) length of orange rickrack trim,
1 inch (2.5 cm) wide

✂ Thread to match fabric and rickrack trim

✂ Small snap fastener

✂ Basic sewing kit (see page 4)

# How to make the wrap skirt

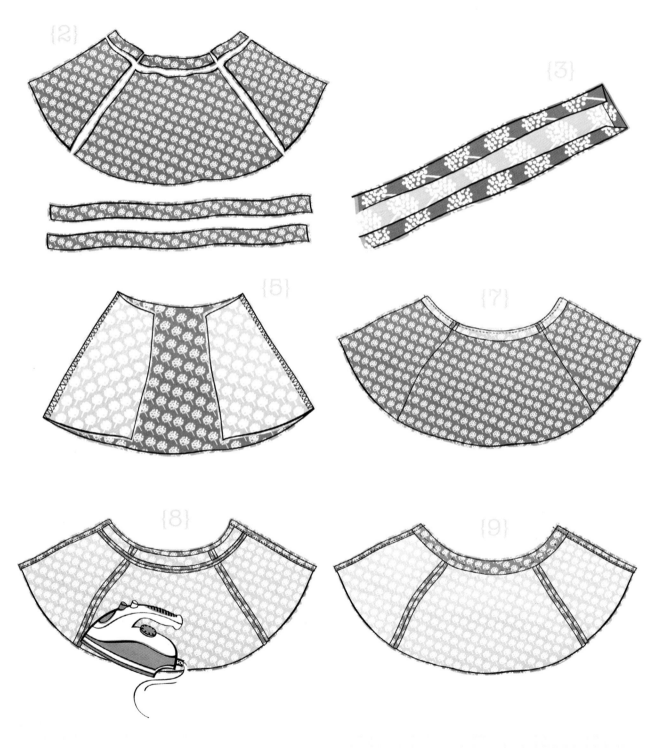

{1} Following the instructions on page 6, make your templates for the skirt pieces.

{2} Cut out all the skirt fabric and facing pieces on the bias (see page 6). Cut one piece for the skirt back in the fabric and the facing by folding back the seam allowance where marked on the templates and placing the folded edge of the templates on the fold of your fabric. Unfold the seam allowance and cut two pieces each for the skirt front in the fabric and the facing. If your fabric has an obvious pattern direction like ours, try to match the design where possible, so that it will face the same way on the finished skirt. Cut out two bias strips, each measuring 1½ x 21½ inches (4 x 55 cm), for the ties.

{3} Fold under ¼ inch (6 mm) along one of the short edges of each tie and press. Fold under ¼ inch (6 mm) along the two long edges and press. Fold the piece in half lengthwise, press again, then machine stitch the folded short edge and the long edges together, close to the edge.

{4} Work a line of zigzag stitching down the sides of the three main fabric pieces of the skirt.

{5} With right sides together, aligning the raw edges, place one front fabric piece on the back fabric piece. Pin in place, then machine stitch the seam, using a ⅜-inch (1-cm) seam allowance. Sew the other front fabric piece to the other side of the skirt in the same way. Press the seams open.

{6} Join the three pieces of the facing together in the same way, using ⅜-inch (1-cm) seam allowances. Press the seams open.

{7} With right sides together, matching the seams and aligning the top raw edges, place the facing on the skirt. Machine stitch the facing to the skirt along the entire top edge, using a ⅜-inch (1-cm) seam allowance. Press the seam open.

{8} Fold in ⅜ inch (1 cm) along the sides of the skirt piece, including the facing, and press. Fold in another ⅜ inch (1 cm) and press again. Machine stitch close to the folded edges.

{9} Fold the raw top edge of the facing down by ⅜ inch (1 cm) and press. Fold the facing down along the seam where it meets the main part of the skirt and press. Pin in place and then machine stitch close to the lower edge of the facing.

{10} With the wrong side of the skirt facing you, insert the first ½ inch (1.5 cm) of the raw edge of one of the ties into the top part of the gap at the top side edge of the skirt. Work two lines of stitching over the stitching already there to secure the tie.

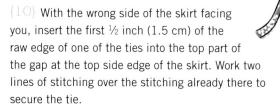

{11} Slip-stitch the tie to the edges of the skirt (see page 7). Slip-stitch the gap in the right-hand side of the skirt closed.

{12} Try the skirt on for fit to decide where you want to sew the second tie. Lay the tie on the waist of the skirt so that the raw edge is on the left. Machine stitch a double line of stitching ⅜ inch (1 cm) from the raw edge. Move the main part of the tie from the right to the left, covering the raw edge, and sew another double line of stitching to secure the tie.

{13} Fold up ⅜ inch (1 cm) along the lower edge of the skirt and press. Fold up another ½ inch (1.5 cm) and press again. Machine stitch close to the top folded edge.

{14} Pin the rickrack trim in place around the lower edge of the skirt, 1 inch (2.5 cm) or so from the lower edge. To make your trimming look really neat, turn over the raw edges of the rickrack and tuck it around the sides of the skirt before you sew it on. Machine stitch a line through the center of the rickrack.

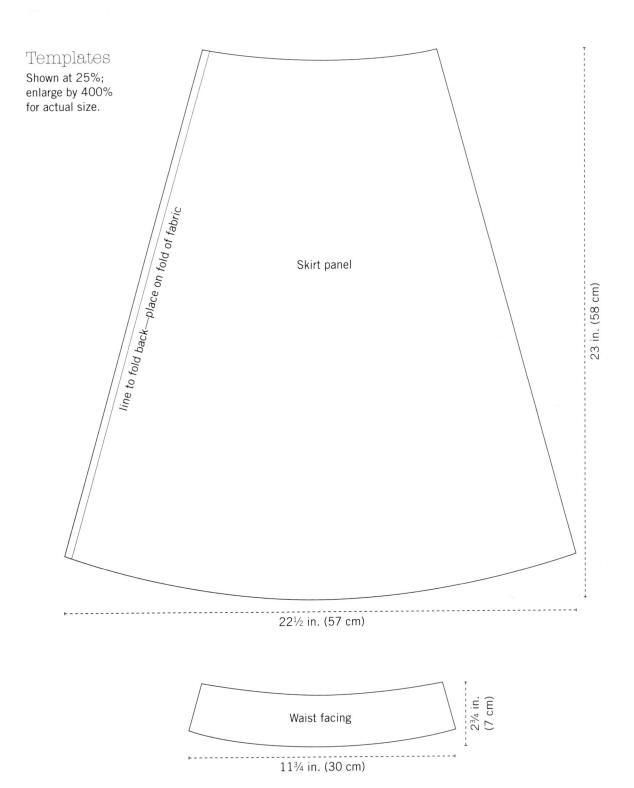

## Templates

Shown at 25%;
enlarge by 400%
for actual size.

line to fold back—place on fold of fabric

Skirt panel

23 in. (58 cm)

22½ in. (57 cm)

Waist facing

2¾ in. (7 cm)

11¾ in. (30 cm)

# Pom-pom-trimmed baby jacket

Every baby needs a jacket or two to look their best when they're out and about. This wrap-style baby jacket is made from a pretty quilting fabric, lined with fleece—and is an absolute cinch to make. We added in a mini pom-pom trim, but you could leave it plain if you prefer, which would make the jacket even quicker to sew. The garment is designed to fit an average-size baby of six months, but you can size the pattern up or down a bit to fit a slightly bigger or smaller baby.

## You will need

- ✂ Templates on page 133
- ✂ Pencil
- ✂ Paper
- ✂ 25 x 42-inch (64 x 107-cm) piece of quilting cotton fabric
- ✂ 25 x 42-inch (64 x 107-cm) piece of cream fleece fabric
- ✂ Sewing thread to match your fabrics
- ✂ 2-yard (180-cm) length of coordinating mini pom-pom trim
- ✂ Two ½-inch (12-mm) snap fasteners
- ✂ Stitch ripper
- ✂ Basic sewing kit (see page 4)

# How to make the
# pom-pom-trimmed baby jacket

{1} Using the templates on page 133, cut out a back piece and a right and left front piece from both your main fabric and the fleece lining. When cutting the front pieces, remember to cut out one piece using the pattern the right way up and one using it face down. Cut the sleeves on both the front and back pieces of the fleece lining ¾ inch (2 cm) shorter than the sleeves on the main jacket pieces.

## A word about fleece

Fleece has a "nap," which means that the fibers lie down in one direction. Before cutting your fleece, check that the nap flows down the length of the jacket. Before sewing, check the right side and wrong side of your fleece; they are similar and it is easy to get them the wrong way around.

{1}

{2} With right sides together, place one of the front pieces of the main fabric on the corresponding part of the back piece and pin in place. Using a ⅜-inch (1-cm) seam allowance, machine stitch along the top of the sleeve and then stitch along the lower sleeve and the side. Clip the curves (see page 7) and press the seams open. Repeat for the other side.

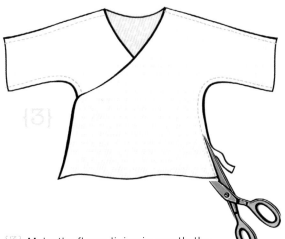

{3} Make the fleece lining in exactly the same way as the outer jacket, but do not clip the curves or press the seams open. Trim the seam allowance to about ¼ inch (6 mm). Turn right side out.

{4} Turn the outer jacket right side out and press. Tack the pom-pom trim to the front and neck section of the main jacket piece, with the line on the trimming where you are going to sew your seam ⅜ inch (1 cm) in from the raw edge and the pom-poms facing inward. Do the same along the lower edge of the jacket. Turn the jacket inside out.

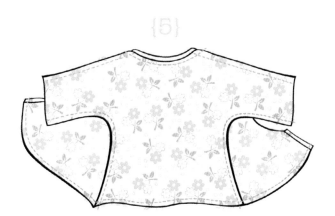

{5} Insert the lining into the outer part of the jacket, right sides together, and pin them together along the neck edge, matching the shoulder seams. Then pin along the lower edge, matching the side seams. Use your machine to sew along the tacking line where you attached the pom-pom trim, stitching ⅜ inch (1 cm) in from the raw edge, then remove the tacked stitches with a stitch ripper.

{6} With the wrong side of the outer jacket facing you, machine stitch along the short front edge on the left front if your jacket is for a girl, or on the short front edge on the right front if your jacket is for a boy, using a ⅜-inch (1-cm) seam allowance. On the opposite side, sew the seam, using the same seam allowance, but leaving a gap of 2 inches (5 cm) in the middle of the seam. You will use the gap in the middle of this side to turn your jacket right side out.

{7} Turn the jacket right side out through the gap. Slip-stitch the gap closed (see page 7). Push the fleece sleeve linings into the main sleeves. Press the jacket lightly only on the outer part.

{8} Fold under ⅜ inch (1 cm) to the wrong side around the cuffs of the sleeves and press. Fold under another ⅜ inch (1 cm) and press again. Insert the fleece sleeve lining under the folded edge and pin in place. Machine stitch close to the folded edge.

{9} Fold the appropriate side of the front over the other front piece, and sew the snap fasteners in place to secure the front of the jacket.

## Templates

Shown at 25%; enlarge by 400% for actual size.

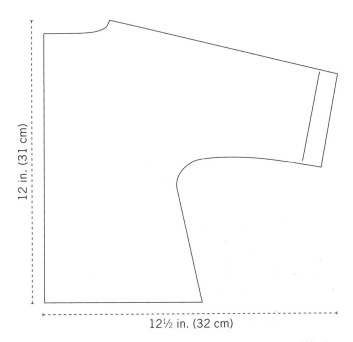

12 in. (31 cm)

12½ in. (32 cm)

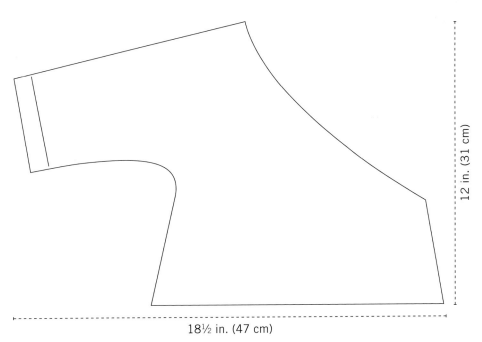

12 in. (31 cm)

18½ in. (47 cm)

# Strapped sundress

A cool, floaty cotton sundress is an ideal pick on a hot summer's day. This one is made from a single rectangle of fabric—with the almost magical addition "shirring," a decorative detail made by stitching rows of elastic sewing thread, which gathers your fabric as you sew. Our sundress has narrow shoulder straps made from the same material, but you could use lengths of ribbon instead, which would make it even simpler to sew. The instructions here are for a dress to fit a five-year-old girl, but you can adjust the size up or down to fit your child.

## Fabric quantities

To work out how much fabric you will need, you will need to take two measurements. First, measure around the child's chest. Then measure from the armpit to the point at which you would like the dress to end. Cut out a piece of fabric twice as wide as the chest measurement and 2½ inches (6 cm) longer than the desired finished length. For my dress, designed to fit an average size five-year-old girl, I used a rectangle of fabric measuring 26 inches wide (66 cm) by 28 inches (71 cm) long. If your fabric has an obvious direction, remember that the pattern should run down the length of the fabric. For the straps, cut four pieces of fabric, each measuring 1½ x 15 inches (4 x 38 cm).

## You will need

- Lightweight cotton for the main dress, plus 6 x 15 inches (15 x 38 cm) for the straps (see box on the left)
- Thread to match your fabric
- Elastic sewing thread; this is normally available only in black or white—choose white for a light-colored fabric and black for a darker fabric
- Elastic, long enough to go around the child's chest and ¼ inch (6 mm) wide
- Small safety pin
- Basic sewing kit (see page 4)

# How to make the strapped sundress

{1} Using your sewing machine, zigzag stitch close to the raw edge of the two long side edges of the rectangle; these are the edges that will form the back seam.

{2} Fold under ⅝ inch (1.5 cm) along the top edge and press. Fold under another ⅝ inch (1.5 cm) and press. Machine stitch just over ¼ inch (6 mm) away from the top folded edge to form the casing. (This will allow you to thread the ¼-inch (6-mm) wide elastic through the casing to make sure the dress fits snugly.)

{3} Wind the elastic thread tightly around your bobbin by hand (if you don't wind it tightly enough, you won't get the right effect, so it's a good idea to first practice with some extra elastic and fabric). Keep your matching top thread for the stitching on the right side of your fabric.

{4} With the right side of your fabric facing you, sew the first row of shirring ⅝ inch (1.5 cm) below the stitching on your casing. Sew another nine rows of shirring, each ⅝ inch (1.5 cm) apart. Keep an eye on your bobbin, because you will probably need to refill it with elastic thread a few times during this process. If your dress is for a smaller child, reduce the number of rows in the shirring. If your dress is for a larger child, add two or three more rows.

{5} Attach a small safety pin to one end of the elastic, then thread it through the top casing of the dress and secure with a few hand stitches at each end (see page 7). Remove the safety pin.

{6} With right sides together, aligning the zigzagged edges, fold the dress in half widthwise. Pin and then machine stitch along the back seam, using a ⅜-inch (1-cm) seam allowance. Press the seam open.

{7} For the hem, turn up ⅜ inch (1 cm) along the lower edge and press. Then turn up ¾ inch (2 cm) and press again. Machine stitch close to the folded edge.

{8} For the straps, fold under ¼ inch (6 mm) along both short edges of one piece and press. Fold the piece in half lengthwise and press. Open the piece out again, fold the two outer edges to the center crease, and press. Fold the pieces in half lengthwise again, making sure the long folded edges line up, and press again. Machine stitch along the long edges, close to the folded edges, and sew along one of the shorter edges. Make the other three straps in the same way.

{9} To work out the best position for the straps, try the dress on the child first and mark the position. Hand stitch the unstitched end of the straps to the inside of the dress, along the lower edge of the casing. On the right side of the dress, hand slip-stitch the strap in place along the top edge of the casing (see page 7).

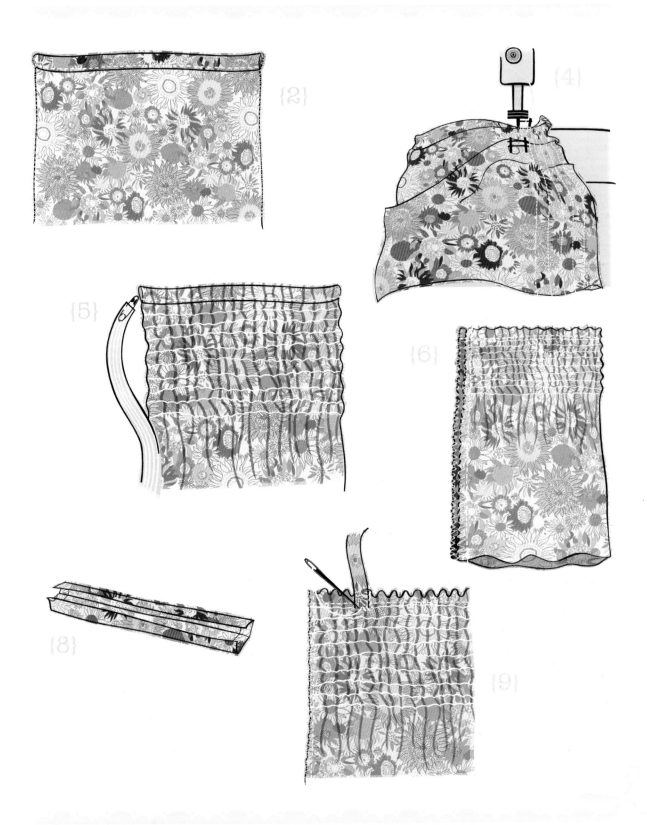

# Pajama pants

Nothing signals the beginning of the perfect evening in as clearly as pulling on a pair of supercomfy pajama pants. And if you're fed up with all the stripes and plaids available in the stores, why not whip yourself or your partner up a pair in a fabric that's, um, a little more interesting? We chose an exuberant cowgirl cotton print—but if that kind of thing is beneath your dignity, there are plenty of other options. Just keep away from those boring plaids and stripes. Despite the drawstring effect, the pants are elasticated for maximum comfort.

## Sizing

These pants are designed to be a fairly loose fit for a gentleman with a 32–35-inch (81–89-cm) waist. The inside leg measures 32 inches (81 cm), which will be long enough for someone around 6 feet (1.8 m) tall when worn slightly below the natural waistline. You can easily make the pants shorter by giving them a bigger hem. You can also make them longer by extending the legs on your template—but remember to allow for extra fabric if you are planning to do so. You can also use the pattern as a guide for making pants in a smaller or larger size, by reducing or expanding the width of the pieces. However, there could be some trial and error involved, so make your first pair using some cheap or recycled fabric.

## You will need

- Templates on page 142
- Tracing paper and paper for templates
- Pencil
- 2¾ yards (2.5 m) cotton fabric at least 43 inches (110 cm) wide
- 39-inch (1 m) length of red ribbon, ⅝ inch (15 mm) wide
- 1 yard (90 cm) elastic, 1½ inches (4 cm) wide
- Thread to match fabric and ribbon
- Basic sewing kit (see page 4)
- Large safety pin for threading the elastic

All seam allowances are ⅜ inch (1 cm)

# How to make the pajama pants

{1} Prepare your templates following the instructions on page 6 and cut them out.

{2} Cut out two back and two front pieces. Cut one piece of the front and back using your template the right way up and one using your template face down. (If you fold your fabric lengthwise before you cut, so that you cut two pieces together, you will automatically cut your pieces correctly.) Cut out two strips to make the waist facing pieces, each measuring 2½ x 23½ inches (6.5 x 60 cm).

{3} Using your sewing machine, zigzag stitch down the sides and crotch curve of all four main pieces.

{4} Pin the two back pieces right sides together and sew the crotch curve. Do the same with the two front pieces. Press all the seams open.

{5} Place one waist facing and the pajama fronts right sides together, aligning the raw edges at the top. Pin and machine stitch together. Press the seam open. Repeat for the back of the pajama pants, using the second waist facing.

{6} Place the front and back pieces right sides together. Pin down the outside of the legs, matching the seams at the waist facing. Machine stitch together and press the seams open.

{7} Pin down the inside legs, matching the seams at the crotch. Machine stitch together and press the seams open.

{8} Turn under ⅜ inch (1 cm) along the raw edge of the waist facing and press. Turn the facing down and press again. Sew the facing in position as close as possible to the lower folded edge, leaving a 2½-inch (6-cm) gap over one of the side seams for threading the elastic.

{9} Attach the safety pin to one end of the elastic, then thread the elastic through the waistband, using care that it does not become twisted. Overlap the ends of the elastic and machine or hand stitch them securely together. Close the gap by continuing the line of stitching that holds the waist facing in place.

{10} Turn under ⅜ inch (1 cm) along the raw edge of the legs at the bottom and press. Turn under another ⅝ inch (1.5 cm) and press again. Machine stitch close to the upper folded edge.

{11} Cut the length of red ribbon into two equal pieces. Place the first piece of ribbon on the "waistband," with one of the raw edges 1 inch (2.5 cm) to the right of the center and with the main length of the ribbon to the left. Machine stitch close to the raw edge. Flip the ribbon to the right, covering the raw edge, and stitch again, close to the fold, to secure. Sew the other piece of ribbon on the other side. Tie the two lengths of ribbon in a bow.

# Templates

Shown at 12.5%; enlarge by 800% for actual size.

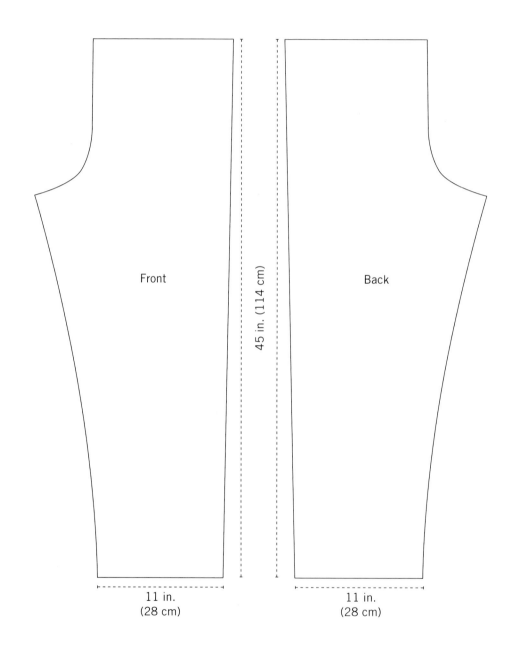

Front

Back

45 in. (114 cm)

11 in.
(28 cm)

11 in.
(28 cm)

# Index

## Acknowledgments

I'd like to thank my sewing students
and friends—Becky, Julie, Karen,
Rachael, Rose, and Puri—for all their
project suggestions for this book. I'd
also like to thank my sister Louise for
accompanying me on fabric-shopping
trips, and my partner Roger and son
Louis for not complaining too much
about living in a house that
resembles a sewing workshop. Last
but not least, I'd like to thank the
editorial and design team at my
publishers for thinking of the idea
for the book in the first place,
and for their skill and patience.